Broken Patterns

BROKEN PATTERNS

by Pat Jordan

DODD, MEAD & COMPANY
NEW YORK

Library of Congress Cataloging in Publication Data

Jordan, Pat.
    Broken patterns.

    1. Athletes, Women — United States.   I. Title.
GV709.J67   796   76-48056
ISBN 0-396-07387-5

FOR LISA, JACQUELINE, AND STEPHANIE

I walk down the patterned garden-paths
In my stiff, brocaded gown.
With my powdered hair and jeweled fan,
I too am a rare
Pattern . . .
Christ! What are patterns for?
                    —AMY LOWELL

Contents

Sweet Home

"Pull over here," she says. The car stops by the side of the road. A sign reads: *Money, Mississippi.* Across the road to the left is another sign pointing down a rutted dirt road: *Sweet Home Plantation.* Up ahead on the paved road is a sagging, unpainted, wood-frame building. A hand-lettered sign dangles from atop its porch: *Grocery Store.* A little farther up the road is a mobile home propped on cinder blocks: *Post Office.* And finally, at the edge of town, stands the tallest building in Money, *The Cotton Mill.*

Parallel to the paved road on the right is a railroad track. Beyond it lie endless rows of green bushy plants flecked with white. A faint morning mist hovers over the plants. She points out the car window toward the cotton fields. "I was born out there," she says. "On the plantation. We lived way down in the fields. Now they build the houses closer to the road, but in those days

1

before anyone had an automobile, they built the tenant shacks in the middle of the fields far from the road. My first memory—I was two years old—is of my uncle leaving home. My mother stood in the yard and watched him walk through the fields. You could barely see the top of his head moving between the rows. When he reached the highway and turned left, my mother said, 'Well, your uncle's leaving home,' and turned and went inside. He walked a few miles down the road to the pink service station—we called it that because it was painted pink—and waited for the bus. He lives in Oakland now.

"I started chopping cotton when I was eight years old. I used a long hoe we called 'the ignorant stick.' At five in the morning the plants were cold and wet, and they soaked your clothes as you moved down the rows. It was a terrible kind of chill. But by late morning the sun would already be hot. Lord, it was hot! You could see the heat waves shimmering behind you and moving up the rows. 'Hurry up,' someone would shout, looking over their shoulder. 'Hurry up, the monkey's coming!' And then others would pick up the shout, 'The monkey's coming, the monkey's coming!' Lord, those rows were long! You could chop for a whole week and never finish a row. I got paid $2.50 a day for twelve hours of chopping.

"I never understood until now why my father made me chop. He wanted me to be independent, I guess, and it worked. I call him my father, but he was really my grandfather. I was born with red hair, gray-green eyes and skin so pale you could see my veins. My real father looked at me and told my mother I was not his child. Three days later he took a boat across the Tallahatchie River from Racetrack Plantation, picked me from my mothers arms and carried me fifteen miles to my grandparents. They raised me. I hold no animosity toward my father. It was just ignorance. Later on he realized that I *was* his child. . . . We can go back now."

The car makes a U-turn in the road and heads south toward Greenwood, Mississippi. It is nine in the morning and the temperature is 92 degrees. Inside the car, however, it is cool, and for a long while the only sound that can be heard is the hum of the air-conditioner. On either side of the road is nothing but endless fields of cotton bordered far off in the distance by a line of trees. Occasionally the car passes a shack by the road or one farther back in the middle of the fields, an oasis in a green desert. All the shacks had once been painted the same color—red—although the paint has long since faded and peeled.

"They always painted the tenant shacks the same color according to which plantation they belonged," she says. "Plantation life was not so bad, really. Every holiday there would be a picnic. They would dig a big hole in the ground and start a fire, then throw a fence over the top of it and roast a whole pig. The owners supplied the food. Each plantation would have its own baseball team, and they would play against each other.

If someone died on the plantation, everyone would stock that person's house with chickens and greens and stuff, and if it was a woman who was left, they would come and pick her crops for her. It was a very warm relationship, really. The hardest adjustment for me to make when I moved to the city was learning I could not be friendly, that you did not sit down beside someone on a bus and talk to them.

"This road was a dirt road when I was a child, you know. People were always walking up and down this road, usually couples holding hands. They walked from Money to Greenwood and back, over twenty miles. They were courting—that is *heavy* courting. Then people got automobiles and then, too, they got afraid when the Ku Klux Klan started riding again. Right over there is where Emmett Till was lynched. You remember Emmett Till, in the 1950s? He was the fourteen-year-old black boy who supposedly winked at a white girl in a drugstore. That night they dragged him from his home and shot him, then wrapped his body in barbed wire and dumped it in the Tallahatchie. I remember once my cousin came to visit and got off the bus at the wrong stop. It was already dark, so she started to walk. Two white dudes drove by. They turned around and came back toward her. She knew what was going to happen, so she ran into the cotton fields and lay down. They searched for her for hours but couldn't find her. She heard them thrashing up and down the rows. It was the most frightening experience in her life, she said. I imagine it was. I never had any bad experiences like that. I try to make arrangements not to put myself in various positions."

The car passes over a bridge that spans the Tallahatchie River and enters the city limits of Greenwood. It moves down a shaded four-lane street divided by a tree-lined esplanade, Grand Boulevard. On either side are massive old mansions long since faded and untended. From the second-floor balcony of one such mansion hangs a Confederate flag.

"They raised me well," she says. "My grandparents, I mean. It was not the same as having parents, of course. They were not affectionate people. I never remembered any warmth from them, any feeling that they really cared, but I never wanted for necessities. And they were strict. Why, they would not let me receive company until I was sixteen. Whenever a boy called the house and asked to speak to Miss White, my mother— my *grandmother*— would answer the phone and say, 'I'm the only Miss White in this house who receives company, and I am sure you are not calling me because I am a married woman.' And they would hang up quick. I appreciate that kind of thing now. It taught me self-respect. But then I just wanted to get out of the house.

"That was why I turned to sports, because it was the only way I could stay out past five o'clock. And I was good at it, too. When I was in the fifth grade I played on the high school's varsity basketball team, and when I was sixteen I was running track for Tennessee State.

Sports was an escape for me too. As a child I was an outcast. Blacks were prejudiced against me because I was so light-complexioned. Parents would not let their kids play with me. They said horrible things about me. In school, whenever there was a play or a dance, the instructors would always choose the little black girls with wavy black hair, starched dresses and patent leather shoes. It did not matter that I could sing and dance better than them. I was too light and I had this funky red hair, and I was always running around in overalls with a dirty face and no shoes. The only way I could get any recognition was through sports. Now those same parents want me to stop by their house, to visit a spell whenever I return to Greenwood. I can't do it. I feel funny. It's not hatred or anything, because I am not a hostile person. But I remember things. Lord, I had a miserable childhood! But I survived. Baby, I . . . have . . . survived."

The car passes over another bridge, much more narrow and rickety than the last. Below it lies the Yazoo River, the color of mud. It smells of mud. It barely flows, seems stagnant. A twig floats in the Yazoo without moving. Across the bridge is Greenwood.

Greenwood, Mississippi (pop. 22,000) lies at the confluence of the Yazoo and Tallahatchie rivers in the lush green heart of the Mississippi Delta, the land of cotton. The city bills itself as "The Cotton Capital of the World" and, to memorialize that fact, has built a tourist

attraction on the outskirts of town that is an exact rep-
lica of a pre-Civil War cotton plantation, even including
slave quarters. Downtown, the city's streets and sidewalks are littered with loose balls of cotton that have
spilled out of the many warehouses and office buildings
that line River Road, which runs parallel to the Yazoo.
Although cotton is no longer the only crop harvested in
Greenwood (soybean is increasingly prevalent), it is still
the most dominate force in the area, as is the mentality
with which it has so long been identified. In front of the
courthouse stands a 1919 statue dedicated to the sons
and daughters of the Confederacy. It depicts a kneeling
woman nursing a wounded soldier. To her left stands a
Confederate sentinel staring through binoculars, to her
right another soldier in the process of drawing his
sabre. Directly above the kneeling woman stands a pa-
ternal Confederate officer wearing a long double-
breasted overcoat. He is staring off into the distance
with aggrieved, pensive eyes.

If the mentality that erected that statue is not so
severe as it once was, vestiges still linger in the townspeople. They have retained the disquieting habit of
narrowing their eyes at the sight of anyone, white or
black, who is not a native son. That narrowed glance is
less physically threatening than it once was—and still is
in nearby Carroll County. Greenwood blacks have a
saying, "It takes a certain *kind* of black to live in Carroll
County." They do not drive through the county unless
absolutely necessary.

Blacks move easily across the railroad tracks in Greenwood that divide the black and white comunities. Blacks shop in town; and they can dine and dance without incident at the Ramada Inn out on I-82 and Park Avenue. Still, there are plenty of white-owned restaurants and bars where, thanks to an underground word-of-mouth cultivated for survival, blacks would never venture. And if those Greenwood blacks are free to move across the tracks during the day, at night they must recross them because they are no more free to live in the white communities that lie west of those railroad tracks than they were fifty years ago. Greenwood, Mississippi, may not be Carroll County, but neither is it the liberal East, which is why it is so astounding that the city, not to mention the entire state, declared March 12, 1972, *Willye B. White Day* in honor of the thirty-two-year-old black woman who once had been afraid even to cross those railroad tracks and who had passed her youth on the plantation pulling "the ignorant stick."

On that day the city was festooned with red, white and blue banners and bunting, and larger-than-life photographs of Miss White. There was a motorcade through the city streets. Miss White rode in an open car and waved to the townspeople lining the streets and shouting her name. The mayor gave a speech in which he declared that the city of Greenwood was proud to have been Miss White's home. She was ushered into the town library, the same library where her grandfather had once been the gardener and she had been denied admittance years before. Inside, the walls were papered with her photograph.

"It was the biggest thing ever in Greenwood," she says today. "You'd have had to live here to understand. As a child I could not cross the railroad tracks; I had to call white children 'Miss' and 'Mister.' And now my name is on every building. My father—*my father,* mind you—got in his truck and drove all day from the plantation to Greenwood just to shake my hand."

Willye White warranted such an occasion because of her achievements in sports, most notably track and field, where she has been one of this country's premier competitors for twenty years. She has held the world's record in the 60-yard dash and the long jump, and has won both a silver and a bronze medal in the Olympic Games. Her fame, however, lies less with any single achievement, record or medal than with the longevity of her career. The fact of having competed for all those years is overwhelming. She has appeared in more Olympic Games—five—than any other "legitimate athlete" in the world. She says of herself, "I have been the grand old lady of track for twenty years." A story in the *New York Times* claimed that "women's track and field began with Willye B. White."

Miss White has traveled around the world twice, competing in track and field in almost every foreign country in the world. Invariably, after she leaves a country she is more fondly remembered as a goodwill ambassador than as a victorious athlete. In the People's Republic of China she was a favorite of both its athletes and citizens, and in Moscow she taught the male Russian athletes how to rock and roll. She has dated Israeli athletes, whom she saw murdered in Munich; she almost married an Italian nobleman; she has kept company with American movie stars such as Bernie Casey, who was once a professional football star.

In 1966 she was named "Fair Play Athlete of the Year" and, along with a number of other athletes, received her award in Paris amid much pomp and circumstance at UNESCO headquarters. A UNESCO official said, "Her poise and charm made her the star of the ceremony." In her native country she has been elected to the Black Hall of Fame in Las Vegas and was appointed to the President's Council for the Investigation of Olympic Sports.

For the past fifteen years Willye White has lived in an apartment on Chicago's South Side. She is a health administrator with the city and works out twice daily in preparation for what she hopes will be her sixth Olympic Games. She is a well-known sports figure (although certainly not so famous as, say, Billie Jean King). She leads the cosmopolitan yet subdued life of an attractive, recognizable, independent, modern bachelor woman. She says of her life, "I can go anywhere, talk about anything. My whole personality has been affected by my travels, which have broadened me. When you are confined to one area all your life you think the whole world is the same."

She is thirty-six years old but has the smooth skin of a younger woman. It is the color of light coffee. Her eyes, also an olive-coffee color, look almost opaque against her skin. She has thick brows and a high, shining forehead topped by a modest Afro hairdo. Her hair is a pale orange which, when caught by sunlight, dissolves into a hazy orange halo. It is one of her most striking features, along with a wide mouth that breaks easily into a dazzling smile. That smile is disarming; it obliterates defenses before they can be properly constructed. At times it is a conscious weapon, at other times merely a natural emanation from within.

Concealed beneath the softness of that smile and her appearance (everything about her—skin, eyes, hair—is soft and pale) is a woman of resilient toughness, but not hardness. Self-assured, in a perfunctory way. She is firm in setting the tone of relationships with people of whom she is unsure. She has consciously cultivated this quality over the years in order to survive on her terms, but it is not something she admires in herself. "When I first came to Chicago," she says, "I applied for a job. I was interviewed by a black man. I asked him if he had anything I might be able to do. He said, 'How about a job as a maid?' I told him that was not really what I was looking for. 'Then say what you want, girl!' he said. 'Don't give people that "I'll-take-whatever-you'll-give-me approach."' He taught me a lot. Being black, I have to be on my toes, to state what I want in a positive way. Whites respect intelligence, authority. I do not necessarily like this approach, but society does not allow me to be any different. I would much prefer society to make offers than for me to make demands."

Once she has set the proper tone of her relationships, she flashes that smile, softening now, and then comes an ingenuous openness. Her candor can first be mistaken for confession, for the seeking of approval and understanding, but eventually the listener realizes it is nothing more than the frankness of a perfectly self-assured person.

Unlike many contemporary blacks, she does not speak an elitest jargon. She uses no code words. Confronted by such jargon once, she said, "Excuse me, but could you please speak English?" She says of such blacks, "Maybe *they* need that kind of thing for identity, but *I* don't." She speaks a perfectly enunciated formal English prose, the written prose of an essay that only rarely would substitute "don't" for "do not." It is not, however, too consciously stylized or devoid of modernisms, such as the phrase "white dudes," which she will occasionally lapse into. In general, though, she speaks the perfect prose one expects to hear from a woman from another time, a woman who is thought a lady. Today such a woman lies outside the mainstream of contemporary life. She resides on an island of the self. That term—"a lady"—is often one of derision in many parts of this country, although once it was highly prized, as it still is in isolated pockets of this land, particularly the South. So, the woman Willye B. White has become over the years is both vastly different from, and inexplicably similar to, the kind of woman she might have become if she had never left Greenwood, Mississippi.

On August 9, 1975, Willye White left Chicago, possibly for good, and returned to Greenwood, Mississippi. She was prepared to surrender her apartment, quit her job, abandon her ambition of competing in six Olympic Games, give up sports entirely, give up her lifestyle of the past twenty years in fact, and return to Greenwood for good in order to nurse back to health the eighty-three-year-old grandfather who had raised her and who was now dying in a small house on East Percy Street.

Miss Willye B., wearing cut-off jeans and a loose-fitting white blouse, sits on a straight-backed chair on the front porch of her grandparents' home and sips distractedly from a can of soda. She raises a hand to adjust the kerchief around her head, which conceals her "corn-rowed" hair, knitted into rows of tight, tiny curls that make her head resemble a furrowed field. She stares with vacant eyes at the street, and says, "Whenever I would talk to him I would say, 'Now Daddy, don't you die while I'm gone, you hear.' These old people, you know, they're like children. He had lost the will to live. I had to come back to give him the will. He had been in the hospital and had not moved for days. He had a 105 degree fever. I stayed up all night washing him with cold towels to bring down the fever.

I hadn't slept in twenty-four hours. The next day he was sitting up, smiling, laughing with me."

She sips from her can of soda, still staring blankly at the narrow street. There is only a dirt curb for a sidewalk. Numerous cars are parked up and down that street in such a way that the wheels resting on the street are elevated higher than those resting on the sloping curb. Any moving car must travel slowly down that street, navigating from left to right to left between the parked cars. The street is lined on either side by houses similar to her grandparents', set close together and close to the road. They are separated from one another and from the road by picket fences. The houses are all alike—long, narrow, unpainted, sagging this way and that like deserted army barracks. The face of each house is dominated by a screened-in porch. Now, at three in the afternoon of a scorchingly hot day, almost every porch is occupied, mostly by older men and women with dark skin and steely-white hair. They stare at the street as if expecting, at any moment, an event. A passing car. Children returning from school. A dump truck delivering dirt.

Parked in front of the house where Miss Willye B. sits are a late model Oldsmobile and a Cadillac, both with California license plates. They belong to her two uncles. The Oldsmobile belongs to the uncle she had seen leave home when she was two years old and had seen only once since then. He is sitting beside her in a straight-backed chair. He is a husky, slightly rotund, dark-skinned man with a gold tooth, dressed in a white t-shirt and worn gabardine trousers. He stares through bifocals at the street. Hanging on the wall between them is a fly swatter. Behind them, inside the house, is the slapping of backless slippers against the linoleum floor. There is the sound of women's voices, hushed, and then the dialing of a telephone, and now a man's voice ordering a tombstone.

"He was a man's man," says Miss Willye B. "In the South, you know, when older blacks are talking to whites they have a habit of taking off their hats. They shuffle their feet a lot and look down at the ground or off to the left, but never into that white man's eyes. My father now—my *grandfather,* I mean—he never took off his hat and he always looked white people right in the eye. When I realized what he did—I was only a child—I began to practice it in front of a mirror. We didn't get along then, he was a stubborn man, but as I got older I realized how similar we were.

"When he got sick I started going back and forth between Chicago and Greenwood, and then I decided to return to stay. It was the first time in my life I had to make such a decision. I could live in Greenwood, you know. Yes I could. It is not the same as it was during the freedom marches. You do not have to fear personal injury anymore. And the other kind of thing I can handle. For example, when my grandfather died I went to the doctor's office to find out the exact cause of death. The receptionist there was very hostile. Finally I said to her, 'Now, listen, Miss, I think we have a misunderstanding here and we had best straighten it out.' We did. I *would* have come back. You see, my parents gave me away when I was three days old and my grandparents did not do a very bad job with me. If they had not reared me someone else would have. I could have been anything—a drug addict, a prostitute. I feel I am what I am today because of them. If I could give them some happiness by coming back to Greenwood, I was willing to do it. I was willing to give up everything I have for them. I have roots. It does not matter how far I have traveled or where I live now. Sometimes I envy the younger athletes. They just take off anytime they want. They never worry about returning home. I would like to be like that sometimes, and then other times I am thankful I do have roots." A fly passes drunkenly before her eyes. She makes a languid, backhanded flick of her hand, and the silver bracelets on her wrist jingle. The back of her hand is prominently veined, and her fingers are long and thin and adorned with many sparkling rings, gems and precious metals of various hues. Her long nails are a frosted pink. Around her neck she wears assorted gold and silver chains and pendants she has acquired over her years of travel.

"God has it all planned," she says. "He does not give you burdens you cannot bear. I was only home a few days when my grandfather died. And then his son came home, he's an epileptic, and he had a fit right on the kitchen floor. He would have died too if it had not been for me. And I said to myself, 'Oh Father! Oh Father! What have you in store for me next!' All I could think of was getting out on the track again and running and running and running and letting the tears come."

Willye . . . runs . . . leaps . . . hangs . . . lands in a spray of sand. She sits in the sand like a child, legs outstretched before her. She looks back over her shoulder at the length of her jump. "Shiiit!"

Behind her, Rosetta Brown, dark, plump, wearing slacks and a jersey, gets down laboriously on all fours and begins to measure the jump with a tape.

Two black youths in their late teens watch intently from the cinder track that surrounds the football field and long-jump pit at Greenwood High School, Home of the Bulldogs. One of the youths is muscular, athletic-looking, while the other is thin, knowing, wearing purple shades. The athletic-looking youth says, "I heard Miss Willye B. was back in training so I come to watch."

Willye takes off her track shoes and stands up. She is about 5′5″, 135 pounds. The muscles in the front of her thighs are so developed they partially obscure the tops of her kneecaps. Her calves are muscular too, although smaller than would be expected. Her stomach is flat. She is wearing a kerchief over her head, a Pan-American Games t-shirt that has been cut off just below the bustline exposing her navel, and tight-fitting track shorts. Her toenails are a frosted pink.

The black youth with the purple shades continues to

stare at her as she dusts the sand off her rump and the backs of her thighs. Finally he says, "My main interest is Miss Willye B., too."

Whenever Miss Willye B. works out she is watched by an army of black youths of all ages. They follow her to the weight room, where she can squat upwards of 380 pounds; then to the football field, where she sprints from goalpost to goalpost, her thick thighs writhing and her knees rising almost to her chin; then to the cinder track where she takes each of the ten hurdles with an effortless leap and a rhythmic crunch of her feet; and finally to the long-jump pit where she concludes her workout. After she leaves each segment of her workout, a few black youths always remain behind to imitate her just-completed feats. They try to heft the weights she had mastered and abandoned, or leap the hurdles she had so effortlessly cleared. When their feet get tangled in those hurdles and they tumble to the cinders, they are jeered and hooted by their cohorts. They laugh at themselves, too, when they fall, because in their mimicry of Miss Willye B. there is no desire to equal or surpass her efforts. They are merely trying to show to themselves and their friends how inadequate they are beside Miss Willye B., the object of their admiration.

Willye White had resumed her training in preparation for the upcoming Pan-American trials and her sixth Olympic Games shortly after the death of her grandfather. Since she had promised her grandmother, a gaunt woman with bony, quivering hands, that she would not leave Greenwood until a tombstone had been purchased and set, she was forced to conduct her workouts at the Greenwood High School field. It was a field she could not have used years ago. But the school has been integrated since then, and now while she worked she can see off on the practice field the integrated Bulldog football team going through their paces under the watchful eyes of black assistant coaches and a white head coach, all of whom were heavy men with generous paunches. The head coach, dressed in Bermuda shorts, was only too happy to make available the school's facilities for Miss Willye B. Of course, he seemed not really to have a choice in the matter: Willye approached him during a coaches' meeting and said, "Coach, I want to use the weight room now."

"Sure thing, Miss Willye."

Walking toward the weight room with the coach, Miss Willye smiles and says with only a hint of a drawl, "Say, Coach, didn't you usta play at Mississippi State?"

The coach lowers his head and says, "Yes, I did, Miss Willye."

"I heard you were *some* kinda football player."

Watching from a distance, Rosetta Brown laughs. "That Red, she's sumthin' else. She gonna have him all over her in another minute."

Willye's workouts are always conducted during the hottest part of the afternoon, and she is invariably accompanied by her childhood friend, Rosetta Brown. Rosetta sets up the hurdles on the cinder track, spacing them just so at Willye's instruction, then rakes and hoes the sand in the long-jump pit as Willye prepares her jump.

At Willye's urging, Rosetta began to train too. Not for any international competition but merely to lose weight. She began to jog. While Willye lopes gracefully over the hurdles, Rosetta, wearing dark glasses and checkered slacks, huffs and puffs her way around the football field with tiny steps. Passing Willye, bent over in pain, Rosetta calls out in a high voice, "Oh, Red! I'm gonna be a traffic stopper again!" and plows on. Willye smiles.

Their lives, once concentric, have long since gone their separate ways. Willye has pursued sports, left Greenwood, traveled, become famous. Rosetta remained at home, married, had five children, saw her husband leave, and so took a job in the cafeteria at Mississippi Valley State University. Once Willye invited her to Chicago. Rosetta stayed only a few days and returned to Greenwood. "I didn't like the city," she says.

"Rosetta has never really traveled," says Willye. "I've experienced things in my life she would never see in her world. Whenever I get the chance I like her to share in some of those things. They are not big things to me, but they are experiences she can talk about for the rest of her life."

Willye White's life may have been a succession of triumphs, but Rosetta Brown's life has not been entirely devoid of victory. She has raised five children on her own, and she once sipped water from an all-white drinking fountain. For the latter she was attacked by police dogs, then arrested. "She was a freedom marcher," says Willye. "I remember the look on the sheriff's face." Willye crosses her arms at her chest, hugs herself while shivering from a fearful chill. "He *oozed* hate! Just oozed out of him. Lord, I could never have done that!

"I look at Rosetta sometimes and think, that could have been me. Sports helped me escape. Sports have made me the person I am today. My mother—my grandmother—was against my being in sports. But it kept me off the street. The time I spent at practice wore me out. If I needed twenty hours of sleep to compete successfully, then I got it. And I learned early that to survive in sports I had to be a thinker. I was better organized than most girls my age. I knew what was best for myself. That is one reason why I turned from sprinting to the long jump. It requires thinking and strategy, not just power. The other reason was that I saw for every 500 sprinters there were only two long jumpers. I played the odds. It was easier. Long jumping is something I could do successfully when I got older. When I was younger I had the talent, the determination, the hard work—and no coaching. Now I have learned more in the last few years than in the previous twenty-five. That is why I am still competing.

"But nothing is forever. I do not expect to jump

forever. Sports have been a part of my life, but not my whole life. I have other interests. The hardest thing for me to do when I quit, for any athlete to do when they quit, is to find some way to fill the hours between four and seven in the evening. Those are the workout hours. But I will be able to quit when the time comes. Some people say I am afraid to quit, that time has passed me by and I am still hanging on. I see athletes I once competed with and they say, 'Willye, when you gonna quit? You're too old.' And I say, 'You are the same age as me, why did you quit?' And they say, 'Well, I got married and I had kids.' 'Well, I am not married,' I tell them, 'and I do not have kids and I am not fifty pounds overweight like you are.' I know my body and its capabilities better than anyone. I am going to sacrifice this year so I can compete in my sixth Olympic Games and win a gold medal. It is my Last Hurrah. They say it cannot be done, that I am too old. But I love challenges. I love to kick society's ass. It will mean more to me now than ever just *because* society says I am too old. Shit, I have been old for a very long time."

On the day before she returned to Chicago, Willye visited the white football coach to thank him for his kindnesses. The coach was standing in the midst of his uniformed players along the sidelines of the practice field, watching intently and shouting instructions to the scrimmaging squad. A few parents, all of them white, stood a little way off watching their sons. Willye, wearing shorts and her cut-off t-shirt, slipped between the players, dwarfed by them and their grotesque shoulders. She tapped the coach on the back; he whirled around and smiled. She said something to him, shook his hand firmly and gave him that dazzling smile. Still smiling, she slipped out from between the players and walked toward the car. The eyes of everyone—players, coaches, parents—followed her for a split second, then returned to the scrimmage. When she reached the car she said, no longer smiling, "Personality, Baby. That is all I got."

She is a platinum blonde yet still attractive, and she is standing in the middle of the one-room Greenwood Airport staring out the window at the runway long since overgrown with weeds and tall grasses. Her arms are folded across her chest and she is tapping one foot impatiently on the concrete floor. She is wearing a chiffony pink dress and white spiked-heeled shoes. Though the thin dress one can see the delicate lace of a full slip. Her hair is bleached and stiff looking, flipped up at the ends in a style favored by Miss America contestants. She has the bold, perfect, nondescript features of a beauty queen, although they are much too heavily made up. Her face is orangey, her brows too sharply penciled, her lips too thickly coated. The makeup seems unnecessary, but she is the kind of woman who prepares prematurely for a loss others have not yet noticed.

It is eight in the morning and she is the only person

in the airport besides Willye White and her companion. Willye is sitting with her back to the same window through which the woman is staring. The woman's gaze never falters, never lowers an inch to acknowledge Willye's presence. Willye is also staring straight ahead, toward the woman, but she seems not to see her either, seems to be staring through that woman to some point far beyond. Willye is talking distractedly to her companion.

"I am glad to be getting back to Chicago. I miss my boyfriend. He is a policeman. I do not date athletes any more. It is a waste of time. Athletes expect you to idolize them, and since I am an athlete too, I don't necessarily think they are a big deal. All of us female athletes have the same problem. We are too independent for male athletes. And then there's the feminity thing. As an athlete you take on certain masculine qualities on the field. Off the field you have to be feminine again. It is not a natural transition. You have to work very hard at it. There is a stigma attached to being a female athlete. If you wear your hair too short and you are always in jeans, the fellas say you are funny. You start getting hit on by certain ladies. That is why I like to wear short dresses and lots of makeup."

Willye no longer looks like the woman sitting on the porch of her grandparents' home. She is wearing a halter top that bares her midriff. Her eyelids and brows are dusted with luminescent white shadow, and her cheeks have a shiny gloss. She has discarded the kerchief that once hid her corn-rowed hair, now fluffed out into a hazy orange ball.

"A female athlete is always two different people," she continues. "A male athlete can be the same all the time. He doesn't have to defend his masculinity. On the track I walk very stiffly, but on the street I make sure everything is moving."

Suddenly there is the sound of a single-propellered airplane. It drowns out Willye's voice. The blonde smoothes the sides of her dress with her flattened palms and walks outside toward the runway. She waits while a small plane taxis up beside her. Its whirling propeller blows her hair back and flattens her dress against her body. The plane stops, a hatchway opens and stairs drop down. The woman puts a foot on the stairs and reaches up with one hand. A disembodied man's hand comes out of the airplane, grasps her hand and helps her into the plane. The hatchway is closed and the plane taxis onto the runway, then is gone.

Without looking back, Willye says with a faint smile, "There is nothing in this world like the White Southern Belle. She has never worked, never done anything, and yet Miss Belle is a proud woman. That one, she was not a Greenwood girl. Maybe she was from Greenwood once, but she has gone to the city. She has got herself a sponsor now. When I was sixteen I had a sponsor. He was a kindly old white man. When he died he left me well. That is why I have been able to pursue my track career all these years. This past week when word got out that Miss Willye B. might be returning to Greenwood I had three offers. A sponsor will bid for you, just like at an auction. You have to make sure you take the best offer. Make sure that the house and the furniture and the car is in your name. You don't want to be sleeping some night and have him come and drive off with your Cadillac. If I had stayed I would have taken a sponsor. That is the only way I could have survived. And I was going to stay, too. Even after my grandfather died. But my grandmother told me she didn't want me. You see, I did not go to his funeral, I just couldn't, and she did not understand."

The door opens. An old black man, wearing a cowboy hat and carrying suitcases in either hand, enters. He is followed by his wife, his daughter and her two children. He puts down the suitcases and takes off his hat. "Good morning," he says to Willye. "How are you this morning, Miss?"

"Fine," says Willye. "Good morning to you, too." In quick succession, his wife, his daughter and her children all say, "Good morning." Then they sit down and wait. The daughter, dressed in a pants suit, sits back and crosses her legs. The children are big-eyed, silent. The old man and his wife are white-haired, with skin as dark as a purple plum. They sit forward on the edge of their seats, as if in anticipation. The old woman is rocking slightly, and the old man, hunched over, is fingering the brim of his hat.

"They are so friendly in the South," says Willye. "In

Chicago I carry a .38-caliber pistol in my purse at all times. Eventually I will come back to Greenwood. I can see myself as an old lady living on East Percy Street. I will get up at five in the morning and go stand on the porch to watch the garbage truck go by. Maybe I will go out to my garden and sprinkle dust on the beans and then go back inside to prepare breakfast, lunch and dinner, all at the same time. I'll piddle around the house for awhile, then maybe I will go back outside to take care of everybody's business on the street. In the afternoon I will sit on a straight-backed chair on the porch and nod. My head will nod step by step down to my chest until I am asleep. That is it. My life."

She falls silent. Her hands rest one on top of the other in her lap. She looks suddenly very small, slight, fragile. And then she begins to smile, that same brilliant, dazzling smile, only somehow different, her mouth pulling down slightly into her jaw.

She is still smiling a few moments later when, in a flat, cold voice completely devoid of inflection, she says, "Life is a bitch, ain't it, Baby?"

Sumthin' for the Imagination

Ma Bass, eyes bulging, head quaking, hands clasped at her chin, kneels on the canvas at center ring under a bright conical light and pleads for mercy. Standing over her is "The Fabulous Moolah," wearing gold lamé tights, who holds her by the hair and cocks a fist. Moolah pauses a moment before delivering a fist to Ma's trembling jaw. In the shadowy corner of the ring behind Moolah, her partner in this six-wrestler mixed tag team match, Dynamite Dick Dunn, is strangling one of Ma Bass's 260-pound sons, Ronnie, whose face is turning purple. In another shadowy corner Moolah's second partner, Tony "The Medic" Gonzales, is standing on top of the ring ropes about to leap off onto the stomach of Ma Bass's other son, Donnie, who lies stunned on his back on the canvas.

Moolah, poised over Ma, turns her face toward the ringside fans at Municipal Auditorium in Pensacola, Florida, and, in elaborate pantomime, seeks approval to belt Ma's jaw. The fans, drawn by a common string, rise as one from their seats, fists punching the air, faces contorted by anger and glee, throats straining and hoarse from shouting, "Kill her, Moolah! Bash the old buzzard! *Please!*" Moolah nods, and her cocked fist shoots toward Ma's jaw. A split second before her fist makes contact, Moolah stamps her foot loudly on the canvas and, simultaneously, Ma Bass's head snaps back and she tumbles backwards through the ropes into the lap of a startled sportswriter sitting on a folding chair at ringside. The fans roar their approval while under the cone light at center ring, The Fabulous Moolah, girl wrestling champion of the world, beats her breast with both fists and lets out an Indian war cry. To her left, Tony "The Medic" Gonzales leaps off the ropes and, momentarily, is suspended in a horizontal diving position before he lands on top of Donnie Bass. His target, however, regains just enough strength to roll over to one side and The Medic lands full force on the canvas —whoomph—on his ample stomach. Donnie Bass struggles to his feet.

Meanwhile, Ma Bass has disentangled herself from the sportswriter and his chair and is climbing through the ropes back into the ring. Moolah races toward the ropes at the opposite end of the ring, hits the ropes, which stretch back like the band of a gigantic slingshot and then snap forward, catapulting "The Fabulous Moolah" back across the ring directly at the dazed and unsuspecting Ma Bass. Before impact, however, Donnie Bass, still groggy, accidentally staggers in front of his mother, and Moolah hits his bulk with a *thwak* and a *whoosh* of exhaled breath. Moolah stiffens, her hands at her sides, then slowly begins falling backward on her heels, like an axed tree. She hits the canvas, bounces once, twice, her arms and legs spread wide. She lies still. Ma Bass falls on top of her and, while the referee slaps the canvas once, twice, three times, the 2500 fans plead for Moolah to get up. But she doesn't, and the match is over.

While Moolah lies unmoving on the canvas, attended to by her partners, Dynamite Dick Dunn and Tony "The Medic" Gonzales, ring announcer Don Griffin climbs through the ropes with his hand-held microphone and, under the cone light, announces the results of the just-completed match. His words are greeted with a chorus of boos. Ma Bass and her sons climb out of the ring and are immediately met by two policemen who escort them through the gauntlet of fans shaking their fists and shouting obscenities. Someone hurls a box of popcorn at the departing Bass family, then some ice cubes, a rolled up program. Now all kinds of debris are falling on Ma and her sons as they hurry, arms folded over their heads, toward their dressing rooms.

Back in the ring, Moolah's partners are rolling her like a log toward the ropes while Griffin, oblivious, consults a piece of paper in his hand and prepares to announce the next match of the evening. He is a bland-looking man in a phosphorescent lime-colored tuxedo jacket and brown trousers that are a bit too short and so expose his white socks and black shoes. He resembles any one of that legion of small-town radio and television personalities—sportscasters, disc jockeys, masters of ceremony—who have never, for some unexplainable reason, made it to Los Angeles or New York City, despite what the local citizens feel is a perfect voice. And Griffin *does* have a mellifluous, if hollow, voice. It is disembodied, seems not to be emanating from Griffin but directly from the microphone in his hand. It is a voice filled with inflection—seems to be, in fact, nothing but inflection, words rising and rolling, dipping and fading, until, listening to him for a while, one tends to grow seasick. Griffin never becomes ill at the sound of his own voice. He pauses frequently between words and cocks an ear as if hoping to catch the last melodic ring of a just-spoken syllable. Often he repeats particularly pleasing words and phrases and purrs pleasurably before continuing. Griffin, in fact, derives great pleasure from the sound of his voice and its ability to impart to his most trivial words a tone of majestic import almost surpassing that of a resent well-known politican addressing a television audience.

"I must qualify my position," he said, before the night's matches had begun. "In my long career as a public-address announcer, I have only been privileged

to work with The Fabulous Moolah twice. And so I
don't feel it is incumbent upon me to comment on her
wrestling techniques . . . techniques. And, suffice it to
say, in my capacity as public-address announcer I am
often called upon to do many things, to wear many hats
. . . many hats . . . and so, seldom do I get the pleasure
of watching the wrestlers perform. However, let me say
this, on those few and far between occasions when I
have observed that well-traveled lady . . . well-traveled
lady, I have seen a truly great ringwise veteran . . . ahhh
. . . ringwise veteran . . . in action. She is more than
worthy of possessing that diamond-studded belt em-
blematic of the world champion. Some people may ask,
and I am not one of them, 'Is wrestling a legitimate
sport?' And I say to them . . . to them . . . you believe
what you want to believe. These men and women have
been down as long and rocky a road as any minor
league baseball player and when that minor leaguer
wakes up one morning in the major leagues he can look
in the mirror and say to himself, 'I paid the price.' Well,
so to is it with wrestling's main eventers such as The
Fabulous Moolah . . . hhhmmm . . . Moolahhh."

Griffin stuffs the piece of paper into his jacket pocket
and then, with a flourish, brings the microphone to his
mouth. For just a moment the microphone wire is
coiled gracefully in midair before falling gently to the
canvas. Griffin leans backward, his spine curved, so that
he seems about to speak to the ceiling, and then in a
booming, hollow voice, announces the next match

while, in the distance, The Fabulous Moolah is being carried to her dressing room by her two partners. The next two wrestlers are climbing through the ropes now. As they do, Griffin is saying, "Originally from Nashville, Tennessee, but now originally from Indianapolis, Indiana, Tommmmm——" and suddenly he whirls around, steps toward one of the wrestlers, crouching low to the canvas as he steps and pointing with a finger "——White . . . White . . ." His voice fades as if an echo.

He straightens up and, with an elaborate flourish of his microphone wire, turns around to introduce the other wrestler, whose face is concealed behind a white hood. He is accompanied by a small red-faced man whose bright orange hair is slicked into a pompador resembling a rooster's crown. The little man is wearing a pink tuxedo jacket and a frilly white shirt. Griffin leans backward again and says to the ceiling, "Identified only as being from somewhere north of the Mason Dixon line, the Mightyyyy——" and again Griffin snaps forward, takes a step, crouching low and pointing "—— Yankee . . . Yankee . . ." He straightens up and adds, "He is managed by that internationally acclaimed manager of top-flight wrestling talent, the irrepressible J. C. Dykes . . . Dykes. . . ." There is a smattering of boos. The little man with the orange hair hitches up his trousers and walks over to Griffin at center ring. Griffin leans over so that the little man can whisper something in his ear. Satisfied, the little man struts back to his hooded wrestler. Griffin brings the microphone to his mouth again and says, "Excuse me, ladies and gentlemen. My apologies. I want you to welcome *Colonel* J. C. Dykes . . . Dykes. . . ." The boos are louder now and continue after Dykes leaves the ring and struts out of the auditorium. With one final flourish of his microphone, Griffin climbs through the ropes, saying as he leaves, "One fall —twenty . . . twenty . . ."

On July 22, her birthday, Miss Lillian Ellison, a fortyish matron from Columbia, South Carolina, steps outside the Hotel Edison on West 47th Street in New York City and, pointing across the street at a pretty girl, says to her gentleman companion, "Looka there, Shuuuuga! The no-bra look! Ain't that sumthin'. You certainly don't see that in Columbia. I jes' don't know. You gotta leave sumthin' for the imagination, don't ya, Shuuuuga? Why, my first husband, he had to look real quick or else he missed it." She goes through a pantomime of unbuttoning her blouse, opening it, then closing it very quickly. "Su-prise! Su-prise!" And then she giggles.

Miss Ellison hooks her arm into that of her friend and they proceed east on 47th Street toward Fifth Avenue, where Miss Ellison has an appointment at Glemby International Beauty Salon to have her hair blown and set by Mr. Maurice. As they walk she says to her gentleman companion, "Did you hear the one about the man and woman who went streakin' in a church. Shuuu-ga? Well . . . she got caught by the fuzz and he got caught by the organ." She puts her hand to her lips to hold back the giggles. "Ain't that cute? I like them kind. They ain't dirty or nuthin', know what I mean? They leave sumthin' to the imagination. A lady always got to leave sumthin' to the imagination. Why, some of these lady athletes, they go paradin' around the locker room in front of one another staaark naked. Now, that ain't decent, Shuuu-ga. Why, when I was a young girl my twelve brothers used to let me play all the games with them, baseball, football, everthin'. They used to stuff me inside an old tire and roll me down the hill into the crik. I was always skinned up. But the only thing they never let me do was go swimmin' with them. I could never understand why."

As Miss Ellison and her companion proceed up 47th Street arm in arm, they are the objects of curious, amused and faintly knowing glances from passers-by. She is a modestly attractive woman in the manner of many small-town housewives—a bit heavy through the middle, but otherwise in fine shape for a woman of her age. She has the small round face and knobby chin of a Susan Hayward, and like Miss Hayward, Miss Ellison wears her wavy black hair pulled back off her forehead and falling to her shoulders. Her eyes are small and narrow and seem to be resting on high and unbelievably prominent cheekbones. A heritage from her Indian forebears, she says. She is three-quarters Cherokee. She is heavily made up—thick pancake base, arched and penciled eyebrows, heavy red lipstick—as women tended to be during the 1940s and 1950s and still tend to be in many small towns throughout American far distant from New York City. Her heavy makeup serves a dual purpose, she hopes: beautification, obviously, and also camouflage for the many small white lines on her face. At first glance they appear to be merely laugh lines, but on closer inspection it can be seen they run against the grain. One such line runs down her forehead, over her left eyebrow and down her left cheek, where it stops. Another runs from the underside of her nose to the top of her lipline.

Miss Ellison is wearing a navy double-knit blazer dotted with white seagulls, a white turtleneck jersey, white double-knit slacks and white platform shoes that add almost four inches to her 5'5" height. She has, in fact, fine, long legs although they are concealed beneath her slacks and by her tendency to take prim quick little steps, her clogs making a clack-clack-clack on the concrete as she walks. She weighs 135 pounds. She will not reveal her age other than to say, "Today is my birthday, Shuuu-ga."

Shuuu-ga is considerably younger, in his early thirties, with an assiduously cultivated tan and wavy black hair. He is wearing light blue sunglasses to match his Pierre Cardin shirt of robin's egg blue. His suit is cream-colored, his shoes brown patent leather loafers with gold tassels and a gold band around each heel. He is still trim in his thirties, looks so obviously pleased with his trimness, while around him other men his age are going to fat. Still, he admits to himself that what he once was at twenty, without thought or effort, he has remained —superficially, at least—only through a painstaking and conscious regime. Alone, he wonders whether the result is worth the effort. It makes no difference. He has no choice. He is one of those people—and this knowledge wearies him daily—who is so conscious of himself, so oppressively conscious of himself in a way Miss Ellison, despite her makeup and her desire always "to leave sumthin' to the imagination," could never be, that he must take great pains to ensure that others view that self only in his desired light. Walking arm in arm with Miss Ellison, for example, he is embarrassed because he knows how those passers-by view him and his companion, chattering beside him.

"Now, my first husband," she is saying, "oh, he was a handsome man. Built just like Joe Palooka, fifty-four-inch shoulders and a thirty-two-inch waist. His name was Johnny Long, and he was sumthin' else, Shuuu-ga, you can take my word. We got along fine at first, but then we had a conflict after awhile. He wanted me to stay home and be a housewife, but I had too much energy for that. I wanted to pursue my profession. It's one of the oldest professions, you know, Shuuu-ga. Really, it is. Why, one night I was on an airplane to Las Vegas and this gentleman beside me kept askin' me what I do that I travel around so much. I told him I was self-employed. 'Really,' he said, his eyes gettin' wide. 'And what *do* you do?' 'I'm just a professional girl,' I said, 'I'm in one of the oldest professions in the history of the world.' He got so excited I thought he was gonna have a heart attack right there in his seat. Well, anyway, gettin' back to me and Johnny Long, one night we was drivin' in his car, havin' this terrific fight, when he up and calls me an SOB. I elbowed him in the face. Knocked out his front plate, I did. He had to stop the car and look for it along the side of the road.

"Now, my second husband, he wasn't bad, but he was no Johnny Long. He called himself Buddy Lee, but really his name was Pino. He was just a little guinea like yourself, Shuuu-ga. Well, when I got married I told my little guinea husband—you know how you guineas are, Shuuu-ga—I told him that I wasn't gonna go lookin', but if I ever caught him with another woman he'd have to pack his bags and git. Well, I did and he did. We'd never got along that well anyway. We lived in the Bronx for a while and I hated it. I guess I'm just a country girl at heart. I looohve the South. I love the clean air and the grass and the trees and the way the wind blows in your hair when you're ridin' a horse. It feels so gooohd. Oh, I just luuuuhv horses. They're like men, Shuuu-ga, but with none of the problems. Well, all the time we was livin' in the Bronx I was pleadin' with my second husband to take me back to the South. But he wouldn't leave. He just went out every night and shot crap in the streets until four o'clock in the morning—ain't that jes' like a guinea, Shuuu-ga? I got sick of it, so one night I packed my bags, got in the car and drove all night until I reached Columbia. I been livin' there ever since. I got a sixteen-room house, thirty acres of land, horses and all kinds of animals, and I'm jes' as free as I can be. I almost got married one other time, too. I was engaged to Hank Williams, Sr., you know, the country-and-western singer who died. I luuuhv country-and-western music. I'm good friends with Jerry Lee Lewis and Elvis Presley and lots of 'em. I got a big ole bass fiddle in my livin' room and whenever they stop by we have a jam session. Man, all night long there's a whole lotta shakin' goin' on. Sometimes, I think if I didn't pursue my present profession I would have been a country-and-western singer."

At Glemby International Beauty Salon Miss Ellison and her companion are met by the manager, Mr. Roy, a slim little man with a large, round, shiny forehead and huge, dark, timid eyes that cause him to closely resemble Tweety Bird. He is wearing four-inch-high platform shoes which, like Miss Ellison's, make a clack-clack-clack on the tiled floor as he walks with quick little birdlike steps to Mr. Maurice. He introduces Miss Ellison to Mr. Maurice, a dour-looking man in his forties. They talk for a moment, Miss Ellison gesturing with her hands and shaping them around her hair while Mr. Roy and Mr. Maurice nod intently. Then they all disappear into another room. Miss Ellison's friend finds a seat against the wall and prepares to wait. The room is done entirely in white and glass and chrome. It is brightly lighted by chrome cone-shaped lights on the ceiling.

Each of Glemby's hairdressers has his own work area—
large mirror, white formica counter, white plastic chair
—spaced out around the room which, this afternoon, is
all but deserted of customers. Seated in front of one
mirror is Mr. Antonio, a darkly tanned, handsome man
who is dressed entirely in white and who resembles a
character from Tennessee Williams's "The Roman
Spring of Mrs. Stone." Mr. Antonio, his black brows
furrowed and intense, is combing out a wig on a white
styrofoam head while Mr. Jon, who looks to be of Ha-
waiian ancestry, sits beside him and studies his every
stroke. Finished, Mr. Antonio holds the styrofoam head
at arm's length and he and Mr. Jon scrutinize it through
narrowed eyes. Mr. Jon shakes his head, no, and Mr.
Antonio returns the styrofoam head to the counter and
begins slashing at the wig with his comb. Seated before
another mirror, Mr. Fausto, wearing a black silk shirt
open to his navel, is teasing the hair on his chest with
a long comb. He examines his chest in the mirror. Satisfied, he puts down the comb and picks up a pair of
small scissors with which he begins to trim the hairs in
his nostrils.

When Mr. Roy, Mr. Maurice and Miss Ellison finally
reappear, Miss Ellison is wearing a gauzy white robe
dotted with red and yellow flowers and her hair is
wrapped in dozens of pink and blue curlers. She
glances at her gentleman companion and then quickly
puts her head down and blushes, as if embarrassed to
be caught in such an unprepared and unladylike state

in which she is leaving nothing to the imagination. She sits down in front of a mirror and Mr. Maurice begins unwrapping her hair and combing it out. Mr. Roy, meanwhile, notices Miss Ellison's companion smiling and he mistakes that smile as meant for himself. He walks over to him and says, "Can I get you a coffee, while you wait?"

"Sure. Thanks."

Mr. Roy walks over to a coffee pot, pours and mixes two coffees and returns. "She certainly is an interesting lady," says Mr. Roy.

"Yes, she is," her companion replies. They both glance over at Miss Ellison, who studiously avoids them.

"She really loves to chew gum, doesn't she?" says Mr. Roy. For the first time, the gentleman friend notices her jaws working steadily and rhythmically.

"You know, you really have to study people in this business," says Mr. Roy. "You have to find out where their head's at, psychologically, that is, sort of get inside their head before you can redo the outside of it, know what I mean?"

"Yes, I think I do. It's very artistic work, isn't it?"

"Very," says Mr. Roy, who narrows his eyes and stares at Miss Ellison's companion. "You know . . ." he pauses, framing the other's head with both hands as if about to shoot a two-handed set shot, "your hair, for example, it could stand some shaping. Yes, I believe it could. I could cut it while you wait, you know. I think I could do wonderful things with it. If you'd like?"

"No, thank you, I don't think so. My wife likes it a little raggedy. I think she'd be upset."

"Oh," says Mr. Roy, and leaves.

When Miss Ellison's hair is finished—teased and sprayed by Mr. Maurice—she smiles broadly into the mirror. She gives Mr. Maurice a ten-dollar tip and thanks him profusely, then takes her gentleman companion's arm and they leave Glemby International and proceed back down 47th Street toward the Hotel Edison. She walks more confidently now, makes little tossing gestures with her hair, and says, "Oh, I feel like a lady again." And then, smiling lasciviously, she adds, "You know, Shuuu-ga, I thought I was gonna lose you there for a minute. Yes, sir. Thought I was gonna lose you," and she throws back her head and laughs.

Miss Ellison goes upstairs to her room to change her clothes. When she returns to the lobby she is wearing spiked-heel pumps, a black-and-white checkered miniskirt that shows off her long legs to excellent advantage, and a silky white blouse buttoned low in front and exposing her more than ample cleavage. She is carrying a small tan suitcase.

"Here, let me take that," says her companion. He takes the bag and is momentarily lurched forward by its contents. "Kinda heavy," he says.

"Oh, is it, Shuuu-ga? I didn't notice. I been carrying it for so long I'm used to it."

Outside, he hails a cab while Miss Ellison stands on the curb. She stands with one foot slightly forward and her hands on her hips. Her back is arched, her chin up, and she is making little tossing gestures with her head. When her companion finds a cab he directs it to 33rd Street, then he and Miss Ellison get into the back seat. Beside him, she smells of lilacs.

"I like the perfume," he says. "What is it?"

"White Shoulders," she says. "It's the only kind I ever use, Shuuu-ga." When the taxi arrives at 33rd Street, an area occupied by the Penn-Central Railroad Station and Madison Square Garden, Miss Ellison directs the driver to the 31st Street side entrance. As the taxi circles the block they pass a vast throng of people ringing the Garden. Old women in faded dresses, middle-aged men in khaki work clothes, not-so-young girls in velveteen hot pants, teenagers in Levis, blacks, whites, Puerto Ricans, Orientals—a bouillabaisse of lower-class Americans, each holding something: a camera, an autograph book with a metal lock, a scrap of paper, a magazine, a photograph, something, as they lounge on the concrete steps, stand in expectant clusters or prowl up and down 31st Street, examining every cab that passes.

"Oh, goodness," says Miss Ellison as they arrive at the 31st Street entrance. Her companion pays the fare, and as he does a black youth sticks his face against the cab window. His eyes grow wide with excitement. Miss Ellison's companion opens the door and helps her out, her short skirt hiking past her thighs. "Hurry!" she says. "Run!" But it is too late. The black youth shouts to the crowd. "Over here! She's over here!" Faces turn toward her, come running from every direction, become a hysterical mob swelling like a tidal wave, rumbling, "Here she is! The Champ! Heh, Champ! Moolah! *Moolah! Mooooolah!*" Hands of every shade and texture, smooth and wrinkled, slap her on the back, reach out to touch her, grab her hand and shake it, thrust pens and paper in her face until her vision is filled with nothing but a sea of hands like fingered snakes and she is truly scared. Finally, a barricade of policemen open an unwilling path, like a swath from the prow of a ship, and "The Fabulous Moolah" hurries in her quick prim little steps toward the doorway, while around her, her fans still shout, "Atta girl, Moolah! Go get her, Champ! We love ya!"

And then she is inside, relieved, and outside the noise is muffled. Faces press around the glass door to catch one last glimpse of The Fabulous Moolah before she boards an elevator that will take her to her dressing room, where she will change into her wrestling tights in preparation for her title bout with Miss Vicki Williams, a twenty-six-year-old platinum blonde from Savannah, Georgia.

In the ring, before 16,000 wrestling fans, The Fabulous Moolah is no longer loved. She is booed and hissed when her name is announced by the public-address announcer, a tall, fat man with a bulbous nose and a beet-red face. Moolah, wearing a black cape, taunts the crowd. She opens the cape to reveal her sequined wrestling tights striped with all the colors of the rainbow. Then, hands on hips, she prances around the ring, shaking her rear end at the shouting fans.

Vicki Williams's name is greeted with a roar of approval since she is younger and prettier in her royal blue tights, and since she is the decided underdog against the The Fabulous Moolah, who has been the woman wrestling champion of the world for the past seventeen consecutive years. Vicki Williams has wrestled Moolah a number of times and has never beaten her. It seems that despite her youth and a devastating dropkick, Vicki Williams is no match for The Fabulous Moolah's unorthodox and less than legal tactics.

Early in the match, for instance, Miss Vicki has Moolah in a headlock, which she manages to break by grabbing a fistful of Miss Vicki's hair and using it to throw her over her shoulder. Miss Vicki lands on the canvas on her back and Moolah kicks her in the head. Then Moolah leaps into the air and lands, with both feet, on Miss Vicki's stomach. She steps off, grabs Vicki by the hair, pulls her, dazed, to her feet and smacks her in the jaw with a fist. Vicki wanders around the ring on wobbly legs. Moolah walks over to her, puts an armlock around Vicki's neck and begins to strangle her while simultaneously gouging out Miss Vicki's left eye. But Miss Vicki, like most professional wrestlers, has marvelous recuperative powers and suddenly breaks free of Moolah's hold. Falling to the canvas, she dropkicks Moolah in the jaw, once, twice, three times. To escape further punishment, Moolah climbs through the ring ropes and steps into the aisle. She pleads for mercy, her hands in front of her face, palms out, as if to ward off an evil spirit. The fans roar approval for Miss Vicki, while a photographer at ringside aims his camera at The Fabulous Moolah, who brushes her hair off her eye, poses, chin up, for a second, and then after the flash climbs back into the ring.

Moolah offers Miss Vicki her hand, vows in pantomime not to play dirty, turns to the audience and pleads with them for understanding. They boo and hiss. Moolah gets down on one knee, crosses her heart and raises her right hand. But Miss Vicki is no fool. She disregards Moolah's protestations and dropkicks her so many times that Moolah's head begins to wobble as if coming unhinged from her neck. Then Miss Vicki grabs the dazed Moolah by the hair and ties her arms inside the ring ropes until she is completely immobile and helpless. Miss Vicki charges at her from the opposite end of the ring, landing full-force with her shoulder in Moolah's stomach. The referee intervenes. Not even The Fabulous Moolah deserves to suffer so, he seems to be saying as he tries to disentangle her from the ropes. Behind him, Miss Vicki charges again, only this time she bashes into the referee, who ricochets into Moolah, and then both the referee and the champion go crashing to the canvas. They roll on the canvas, a tangle of thrashing arms and legs, while the fans laugh and cheer. Moolah flails at the referee, is soon sitting on his stomach punching him with her fists. Finally she leaps up, brushes herself off and tosses her head back with disdain, as if her dignity as a lady had been violated by something the referee had done while they were intertwined on the canvas. The fans hoot her demeanor; someone calls out, "You wish, Moolah!" She turns, menacing, toward the crowd.

Near the end of their championship match, Miss Vicki manages to get Moolah's shoulders pinned to the canvas by virtue of a leg hold around her neck. The referee slaps the canvas once, the fans roar. He slaps it twice, the fans rise from their seats, screaming with anticipation at this upset in the making. But suddenly, with devastating speed, The Fabulous Moolah reverses the hold. Now it is Miss Vicki Williams whose shoulders are pinned for a count of one, two, three, and the match is over. Moolah still reigns. The fans, their hopes dashed with such blinding rapidity, are stunned, silent, as Moolah leaves the ring.

At midnight, in the back seat of a taxi heading toward Jimmy Weston's Supper Club on East 54th Street, Miss Lillian Ellison says to her male companion, "I was always a good athlete, Shuuu-ga. When I was a girl back in Columbia I used to go to them County Fair Days and win all the medals in track, high-jumpin', everthin'. Most of the times I beat the boys. Like I told you, I had twelve brothers and I followed them everwhere, did everthin' they did, except of course go swimmin'.

When I was about eight my mother died and, to help me forget, my father used to take me to all kinds of events. One night he took me to my first wrestling match, and the minute I saw those girls I said to him, 'I'm gonna be that . . . a lady wrestler.' Well, I wanted to wrestle so bad that when I got to high school I started houndin' the boys' wrestlin' coach. He said they never had no girls on the team before. I said that don't make no difference to me. Finally he had to let me on. Why? Because he just couldn't stop me, that's all. I wrestled my last two years in high school, mostly against boys, and I beat 'em, too. When I graduated, one of my brothers, who was a Golden Gloves fighter, won a trip to Johannesburg, South Africa. For my graduation present my father asked if I'd like to go with him. I said, 'I certainly would.'

"In Johannesburg I met this wrestlin' promoter named Tiger Simpson and I began houndin' him for a match. 'You don't know enough,' he said. 'I'm willin' to learn,' I said. Then he said, 'Why you wanna wrestle, girl?' And I said, 'Mr. Simpson, we had thirteen children in my family and we had to fight for every biscuit, man, so I just gotta make some money.' Then he looked at me real close—I only weighed about 110 pounds—and he said, 'You're awful small to do that.' I said, 'I'm small, Mr. Simpson, but I'm mighty.' Finally he just had to give me a chance. But before my first match he said, 'We're gonna have to do sumthin' about that name of yours. Lillian Ellison, that don't sound like no wrestler.'

'I don't care what you call me, Mr. Simpson,' I said, 'so long as I can wrestle and make some money.' He thought a minute and then said, 'You wanna make some moolah, huh? Do you mind if we call you Slave Girl Moolah?' 'Certainly not,' I said.

"Well, I wrestled there for a while and then I returned to the States to get my first real big match. I weighed 118 pounds by then, but in those days most lady wrestlers were *big* girls, and when I went to fight in Boston I couldn't pass the weight test. The promoter there told me to go home and forget about wrestling. He said I probably would never get a match unless I was at least 138 pounds. I told him I'd be back. I went home and started eatin' steak and mashed potatoes with butter. Every morning and night I drank a glass of pure cream with two tablespoons of Hershey syrup and three raw eggs. How'd it taste? Guuuuhd, Shuuu-ga, 'cause it was gonna help me be a wrestler. Well, one day I called back that promoter and said, 'Mr. Wood, you don't remember me, but my name is Lillian Ellison. I'm that little girl you said should forget about wrestling and become a secretary sittin' on somebody's knee. Well, I weigh 149 pounds now, and I wanna wrestle.' He said, 'O.K.,' and I been wrestlin' ever since. At first I wasn't real successful. I was too gentle 'cause I wanted everyone to love me. But after I lost a couple I said, 'Heh, this ain't me, I gotta be like I was with my brothers.' Well, when I finally started to let go, I started winnin' most of the time. I learned that in wrestling you could act the way you feel, which you can't do in regular life. I mean, you wake up one morning and feel wild or sumthin', but you can't let yourself go. Well, when I'm wrestling I always let myself go. Of course, there are rules, but most of the time I lose my head and I don't follow no rules if I can help it.

"Well, anyway, I finally won the championship one night in Baltimore. It was the most fabulous thing you could imagine. They just put thirteen girls in the ring and let 'em all wrestle at one time. I beat 'em all, and then after that I had to wrestle the champion, June Byers. I beat her in two straight falls, and I've been the champion ever since. After I won that night, the Maryland State Athletic Commission told me that my name, 'Slave Girl Moolah,' was a little misleadin' and would I please change it. I was so happy I would of changed it to anything. They said, 'Well, you beat thirteen girls in one night and that's pretty fabulous, so maybe we'll call you 'The Fabulous Moolah.' I was nineteen.

"Why do I do it? I luuhv it, Shuuu-ga! I love to travel, I love the money and I love meetin' people. And in the ring I can let myself go. You know, be myself. Of course, there's always the risk of gettin' hurt. I had my neck broke in Denver once when a girl jammed my head into the mat. I still have to go to a chiropractor for it. I've had just about all my fingers and toes broke. See this scar above my lip? I got that when a girl rammed my face into the side of a turnbuckle, the metal buckle that keeps the ropes up. Another time, a girl rammed my head into a turnbuckle and it cut me from my forehead down over my eye all the way to my cheek. See here! I don't know how it missed tearin' my eye out. Probably the worst thing that ever happened to me was the night a girl jumped on my stomach and almost ruptured my spleen. They had to rush me to the hospital, and I thought it was curtains for me. But that's about the worst thing I can remember, except for that time in Oklahoma City when I was knifed by an Indian. I was wrestling this full-blooded Indian girl named Celia Blevins and after I beat her and I was walkin' toward the dressing room this big Indian guy —he was the biggest man I ever seen—come at me with a knife. I started backin' up, and then he took a swipe at me, cut me right here on the shoulder, before the crowd closed around him and I could get away. Another time, in Colorado, I got into a fight with the ring announcer. He pulled my hair and I threw a chair at him. In Holyoke, Massachusetts a few years ago a fan reached into the ring and pulled me by the hair, so I kicked him in the face and broke his jaw and nose—it went way over to one side of his face. Oh, it looked pitiful. In Dallas, Texas, another night I was half-knocked out in a match, and when I came to my senses, five cops was trying to pull me outta the ring. I was kicking, punchin', ever'thin, and they couldn't do nuthin' with me. Sumthin' like that kinda scares you. You wonder. But still, I luuuhv wrestling. It's been guuuhd to me, Shuuu-ga. I hope I don't ever lose my title. Never. My God, this is the best I got."

Parked outside of Jimmy Weston's Supper Club is a
long, seemingly endless line of black limousines—
Cadillacs, Continentals, Mercedes and Jaguars. Uniformed chauffeurs mill about on the sidewalk, lean
against their cars smoking cigarettes and talking softly
while, inside, their employers are having a midnight
supper and half-listening to the singing of a soft, fat,
light-skinned Negress dressed in a frilly white plantation dress and who was once, it is claimed, the wife of
Adam Clayton Powell. Inside, Miss Ellison and her companion are escorted by the maître d' to a long table
occupied by Vince McMahon, a multimillionaire wrestling promoter, and his party of twelve. Mr. McMahon,
tall, gray-haired, ruddy-faced, half-rises from his seat to
greet Miss Ellison and to introduce the two of them
around the table. Miss Ellison smiles warmly at each of
the guests, who look up and nod perfunctorily. Miss
Ellison sits down beside Mr. McMahon, who says,
"Good show tonight, Lil." She blushes and thanks him.
A waiter appears, asks for her order. Momentarily flustered by such attention, she mumbles, "Just bring me
what everyone else is havin', please." To Miss Ellison's
right, Mr. McMahon returns to his conversation with
Willie Gilzenberg, a halting, white-haired old man who
is president of the World Wide Wrestling Federation.
They are discussing the night's attendance at Madison
Square Garden and the prospect for a future promo-
tion. To Miss Ellison's left, Mr. McMahon's son, a massive 6'3" 250-pounder who is referred to by everyone

as "Junior," is discussing the relative merits and deficiencies of his $27,000 Ferrari Daytona GTB-4 with his neighbor, Billy Mack, a quick little man with a sunlamped tan and six inches of French cuffs. Mr. Mack, speaking out of the left side of his mouth in a Bronx accent, informs "Junior" that he has no interest in his car but would prefer to talk about Evel Knievel's Snake River Canyon jump, for which "Junior" has the exclusive closed-circuit television rights. "How much do ya think it'll bring, ya, Junior?" says Mr. Mack.

Momentarily ignored, Miss Ellison turns to her friend, who, not having eaten all day, is busily stuffing shrimp and clams oregano into his mouth. She leans over and whispers into his ear, "This talk is sure too deep for me, Shuuu-ga." He nods and continues eating.

Throughout dinner Miss Ellison is strangely subdued, deferential almost, in marked contrast to the braggadocio and confidence she exudes in the ring. It is an honor to be invited out to dinner with these wealthy people, she tells her companion. Wrestlers don't usually socialize with their promoters. "But these people are so down to earth," she adds. "Mr. McMahon is just the most natural person. He's a personal friend of mine, really. And besides, he knew today was my birthday."

When Miss Ellison is finished eating she puts down her knife and fork and for want of something better to do with her hands, she begins to tug and twist her napkin on the table. Catching herself, finally, she stops. She folds the napkin with great care until it is a very tiny square which she puts on her lap. She then lays her hands over the napkin, arches her back slightly and, after making a little tossing gesture with her head, sits there silently. A waiter appears to clear away the dishes. Moments later he reappears bearing a white cake with a single candle burning in its center. He stands in front of the table waiting direction. No one notices him. He clears his throat. Mr. McMahon, deep in conversation, looks up and motions toward Miss Ellison. The waiter deposits the cake in front of her and leaves. She is stunned, her eyes wide with disbelief. She flattens her hands over her lips as if to stiffle a gasp. "Oh, Vince!" "Happy birthday, Lil," he says. From around the table, heads look up, smile briefly. There is a smattering of "Happy Birthdays," then a return to conversation. Miss Ellison sits there, staring at the burning candle, its flame reflected in her eyes, illuminating the thin white line running over her left eyebrow and down her cheek. Her face is deeply tanned and the white line stands out clearly like the line of a river drawn on a weathered map. Caught in the crevice of that line is a tear.

Would I Do It Again?

Wearing jeans and ski boots, Anne Henning, nineteen, a sophomore at Carroll College in Waukesha, Wisconsin, sprawls on the cot in her dormitory room and watches with wonder as her roommate, Sheila, wearing creamy slacks and a silky blouse that rustles when she moves, flutters about the room. Sheila lights for an instant, flutters off, lights, flutters, a fragile and beautifully marked butterfly trapped in a jar. She lights before a mirror, yanks a comb through her hair, then flings it to her cot. She moans out loud, "Oh, I'm totally flipped!" and escapes the room.

Anne Henning shakes her head and smiles. She is wearing no makeup. She has wide, direct blue eyes, pink cheeks, a small mouth and a cherub's head of tight fluffy golden curls. She says of her roommate, "She fascinates me! Really, we've been roommates for two years and no one can understand why. She's so scattered, hysterical almost. And me, well, I just sort of drift. Still, I wouldn't have any other roommate. I'm hypnotized by her. Last year she was terrified of me. She wouldn't go swimming with me, or toss a football around, or go skating or anything. She was afraid she'd break. This year she's changed a lot. She'll do sports now. And she tries so hard. It tickles me. One day I ran four miles and she tried to run with me. She kept up, too, although she walked most of the way. When we got back she was black and blue. Would you believe it? From walking! I never talk sports around her. If I do she puts cotton in her ears. I laugh. I call her Miss Ultra-Femininity. She changes her clothes four times a day! In the morning on the way to class she looks like she just stepped out of *Glamour* magazine. But she doesn't do it to show up anyone. It's just her nature. I don't feel threatened or anything. There's no competition between us. We're just fascinated by each other. We never experienced anyone like one another before. I think she's so cool. Really! If I could be like her I would. But I'm not. I never was a teeny bopper. I was a child and then an adult. I missed that growing-up period in between."

From the age of ten until she turned sixteen, a period during which most young girls are cultivating the trappings of femininity (fragile flutterings one assumes come naturally but which, in reality, are acquired through conscious and diligent imitation), Anne Henning was devoting all her energies and concentration to becoming the fastest woman skater in the world. As a child in Northbrook, Illinois, a suburb of Chicago, she excelled in all of the usual sports. Often she competed successfully against boys her own age, although those successes were confined to casual pick-up games at the local park. She was prohibited, by her sex, from competing against those same boys in more officially sanctioned contests such as the local Little League program. "That didn't really bother me," she says. "I knew I could beat the boys, and they knew it, too."

One of the few sports in Northbrook in which Anne could compete on an organized level was speed skating. The town had an excellent speed-skating program thanks to the efforts of Ed Rudolph, then the park commissioner and a world-class speed-skating coach. Anne quickly gravitated to the sport, partly because it was accessible to her in a way baseball wasn't, partly because she discovered she had a talent for it (powerful legs), but most of all because of Rudolph, whom she would later describe as "more understanding than any adult I know."

An easygoing man in his fifties, Rudolph was the first person to recognize Ann's talent for skating. He first saw her skate when she was ten years old, and said to himself, "She's a genius! She's born for it!" He recalls, "I saw nothing but gold medals dancing before my eyes."

Rudolph immediately told Anne and her parents (her

father, Bill, was a hospital consultant and her mother, Joanne, a nursery school teacher) that she had the potential to become an Olympic champion. She needed only to hone that talent through a few years of diligent practice under his tutelage. "It won't be all fun and games," he told them.

What Rudolph was saying, in effect, was that for the next six years Anne's life would be almost totally dominated by her sport. And that, in the process, her life would be profoundly influenced by him. Often, thousands of miles from her parents, Anne would be responsible only to Rudolph and to herself. Although neither of her parents was particularly compulsive about Anne's sport, they were both impressed with Rudolph, and so they acquiesced to his and their daughter's wishes. Said her father at the time, "We just want Anne to skate only as long as she enjoys it. If she needs our support, we're here to give it. This is sport—not a lifetime career."

Under Rudolph's gentle prodding, Anne began, at the age of ten, a training routine that included four hours of practice every day of the year. By eleven she was making weekend excursions to various parts of the country in order to compete on the level of her burgeoning talent. At the age of twelve she won the U.S. National Championship in both the 500- and 1000-meter events. By her fourteenth birthday she was spending most of the winter months in Europe, skating, in international competition.

"I'd go to school only in the spring and the summer," she says. "I didn't skate during that period, but all I thought about was skating. I'd work out a lot, do sprints and special exercises Mr. Rudolph had got from Europe. I was very careful not to play any sports in which I might sprain an ankle. As soon as winter came, I left for Europe. I loved it. I thought it was the neatest thing in the world at the time. I was completely responsible for myself. I made my own decisions for the first time in my life. Sometimes, though, I would get discouraged. I was always off someplace skating while my friends were running around Northbrook. They never knew where I was and I never knew what they were doing. Maybe if I had realized what fun they were having, I might have quit. I threatened to quit once. I was kind of bitter toward Mr. Rudolph for making me do things, although he was never one of those really strict coaches. But I'd always hated to train. For a while I wouldn't go out to practice. Then my parents and Mr. Rudolph sat down with me and let me see how close I was."

Shortly after her fifteenth birthday Anne set world speed-skating records in both the women's 500- and 1000-meter events. A year later she was in Sapporo, Japan, competing in the 1972 Winter Olympic Games. She was considered, by most objective observers, to be a shoo-in for gold medals in both the 500 and 1000 meters.

"There was so much pressure on me," she says today.

"I was the world record holder in both the 500 and 1000, so people just naturally assumed I'd win those events. 'She's no problem,' the U.S. officials would say. 'She'll win her two, so we can concentrate on the others.' That just burned my mind! I didn't need any attention! You know, they just put me in a little box, 'Here's a fast speed skater, send her out to win, that's all there is to it.' I was *supposed* to win. They never took the time to think how much that pressure was taking out of me. I was only sixteen. But to them I was just a . . . a piece of . . . you know . . ."

Although Anne Henning did win her expected gold medal in the 500 meters (setting an Olympic record in the process), her victory was not without incident. Midway through her heat, as she and her opponent were taking a curve neck-and-neck, they almost collided. To avoid contact Anne stood up and let her opponent pass, then skated after her. Although Anne eventually passed her and won the heat, she had lost precious tenths of a second from her time. She feared that other girls, notably the Russians, would better that time.

"I was so upset I wanted to go home right then," she says. "I never wanted to skate again. But the judges decided that I had been fouled and so, twenty minutes later, I was given another chance. I knocked four-tenths of a second off my time, which was good enough for the gold medal. Of course I learned later that my first time of 43.7 would still have been good enough to win."

The following day, mentally and physically drained from her experience, Anne finished third in the 1000 meters and, to the disappointment of many U.S. Olympic officials, received only a bronze medal. ("I was never disappointed in anything I did," she says today. "I was just thankful I'd won something and it was over.")

Immediately after she finished her heat in the 1000 meters, before she managed to catch her breath, Anne was approached by a U.S. Olympic official. He commiserated with her on her third-place finish and then, referring to the World Games to be held later that winter, said, "Well, anyway, we're on to Sweden. We can win there."

Without thinking, Anne blurted out, "Right. Sure, we can win in Sweden. Only I'm not going."

Sprawled on the cot in her dormitory room, Anne says in a soft, barely audible voice, "I had every intention of going to Sweden. I never thought of *not* going. It just came out. I was tired, I guess. Worn out at sixteen. I'd packed a lifetime of energy into six years and I didn't have any more left." She smiles, gestures languidly with a hand. "I still don't." She is nineteen now and has not skated competitively since the day when she finished third in the 1000 meters at the Olympic Games.

Hanging on the wall in her room is a small photograph of herself at sixteen. She is wearing a ski cap

pulled over her ears and a navy sweat suit. Her cheekbones, nose and jaw are sharply defined and glistening
with sweat after a just-completed workout. Her naturally curly hair is wet too, and it hangs like yellow string
about her face. The girl in the photograph bears only
a faint resemblance to the one in the room. Possibly it
is just the hair. Her now fluffy golden curls ring her face
like a halo, soften its focus, make her straight, perfect
features less sharply defined. *She* seems less sharply
defined. She is devoid of sharp edges, smiles easily,
gazes directly into one's eyes, not judging, not analyz-
ing, but just looking with wonder. She is not trapped in
a jar of self-consciousness, possesses none of those false,
fragile flutterings that clutter up the natures of so many
of her sex. (One night, Anne and her roommate are
invited out to dinner by a friend. Sheila, with flair, or-
ders a cocktail, "A Moité, Moité, please," while Anne,
wide-eyed and smiling, says, "I don't believe you did
that! Wow!")

  "I was always going at such a fast pace," she says,
"always going someplace special. Finally, I just wanted
to slow down, to lie back and be normal for once. I felt
at that time in my life I wanted to see new things, to
enjoy being and doing what I wanted to. I told Mr.
Rudolph I didn't want to spend the rest of my life training and, now, I didn't have to if I didn't want to. I could
still be skating for the next Olympics, but what for? I've
done it. I had a natural talent for something, it was
within my grasp, and I achieved it. I'm proud of what

I did. But so what? I don't want to wear it out. I have no need to be always recognized as a star. I'm satisfied with myself. I don't need people telling me what I am, what I did. I know. Once I skated faster than anyone else in the world. It didn't make *me* great.

"Since I've stopped skating I haven't found anything to interest me like skating did. I'm glad. I don't want any goals right now. I want to drift. I never had a chance to just drift when I was growing up. Oh, I still play sports, but it's different now. I do everything— baseball, football, swimming—and I don't have to worry about getting hurt. I'm on the girls' track team. But it's just for fun. I don't care if I win or lose. It tickles me how serious all the other girls are, though. I run a lot on my own, too. Why? No reason, I just feel like it sometimes. One morning I got up before dawn and ran six miles. It was below zero and the snow was up to my knees. I saw the sun come up over the horizon. I love horizons. When I got back to the room Sheila said I was crazy. I told her I was just a dumb athlete.

"I owe a lot to sports. If I didn't get into athletics I have this feeling, I don't know why, but I just do, that I wouldn't be too neat a person. I'm lazy. I couldn't care less what I do, what people think. That's something that haunts me. I always try to find the easy way out. I don't want to be here in school, for instance. I don't feel it's the right time in my life to be tied down again. I want to go back to being younger, when you can drift a little. I have this feeling that I missed a part of my life I'll never be able to recall. But society won't let you go back. You're supposed to be what you are at a certain age. So here I am in school. I'm still taking the easy way out, though. I'm an art major. It's just talent, like skating. What am I saying? I don't have any talent for art. . . . I don't know how long all this will last." She makes a sweeping gesture with her hand. "I'm dissatisfied so easily. I've seen so much, Europe and all, I don't ever think I'll be satisfied with the things I might have if I didn't get into sports. I know there are things I can have and be, which I never would have realized if I hadn't gotten into athletics.

"Would I do it again? Nope."

The Penn State Girls

GETTING HIGH

There is the sound of a cello—soft, slow, somber. It fills the room, which is bright with polished chrome and glass and white paint and overhead lights that cast no shadows below. It is a large room, perfectly square and unusually high-ceilinged. Atic mirror against one wall rises almost to the ceiling. Standing at the base of that mirror is a slight Oriental girl wearing black tights. She is poised on the toes of one leg as if about to pirouette. She stares at her image in the mirror for a long moment, her arms forming a halo around her head, her legs forming a perfect figure 4, then slowly, on the point of her toes, begins to turn.

Dominating the center of the room are the gymnast's uneven parallel bars, the polished chrome catching light and images and reflecting them in silver slivers. Standing on the higher bar, her legs spread wide for balance, is a short, muscular girl in powder blue tights. She is tying a heavy towel around her abdomen, which has begun to swell from the force with which it whacks the lower bar when she performs her routine. Beside the uneven parallel bars is a balance beam, a long, smoothly-finished, log-shaped piece of wood supported about four feet off the ground by chrome-plated legs. A girl in pink tights is standing on her head on the beam. She is extremely tall, thin, long-necked. Her legs are spread wide, like opened scissors, and she is using her hands as feet to make a 180-degree turn on the beam.

Running parallel to another very long wall is a black, ruglike mat about three feet wide. At one end of the mat stands a tall woman in her early twenties. She has long, straight blonde hair, pale almost translucent skin, and fine fragile features constructed of bone as delicate as tissue. Both in appearance and demeanor she resembles Dina Merrill, the debutante-actress. Wearing dark slacks and a turtleneck jersey, she is standing with her chin thrust forward and up, her hands on her hips, one leg slightly advanced. She taps her toe impatiently. Behind her is a gymnast's horse, a polished piece of wood about the size and shape of a horse's trunk. Still tapping her foot, she calls out, "Anytime, Karen."

At the other end of the mat, fifty feet away, is a younger girl wearing purple tights. She looks 5'5" tall and 120 pounds, some of which spills out of her tights at the thigh. She seems heavy for a gymnast, a little too soft. She is standing perfectly still, her head lowered and her eyes closed as if lost in the sounds of the cello, or maybe prayer. Her arms are rigid at her sides, fists clenched, legs pressed tightly together. "Whenever, Karen," calls the blonde woman, Judi Avener, the women's gymnastic coach. As a Springfield College undergraduate, Judi Avener was a college All-American gymnast at the age of twenty-one, which, in gymnastic circles, is comparable to being a thirty-four-year-old all-star shortstop in the Florida State League. Truly great gymnasts, such as Judi Avener's husband, Marshall, are members of the Olympic team in their mid-teens. Marshall Avener was an Olympian twice. A quick, twitchy, loquacious little man, he resembles in everything but size a character played by Tony Perkins. He is the assistant coach of the men's team at Penn State and often will assist his wife at her practices, or take over for her when she is busy elsewhere. "It's ironic," he says, "I was an Olympian and she was just an All-American, and now *she's* the head coach."

Like Marshall Avener, Karen Schuckman, the girl in purple tights at the other end of the mat, was also an Olympian, at the age of fifteen. For ten years her life was devoted to her sport until, at the age of sixteen, she retired from competition. She returned to gymnastics when she enrolled at Penn State in 1973 as an Asian Studies major, and shortly thereafter became one of twenty women athletes to be granted an athletic scholarship, the first such scholarships in the school's history.

As a freshman, Karen Schuckman was undefeated in women's collegiate gymnastics. She is the most visibly successful of all the scholarship women, and she is the first to receive national recognition. She thinks little of her achievement. "We used to laugh at college gymnastics when I was fourteen," she says. Because of Karen's background, Judi Avener is often deferential to her star gymnast, something that at times rankles Judi. It is a question of the modestly talented coach and the genius pupil. During practice Karen Schuckman works at her own pace, in her own private world. She calls her coach "Judi."

Karen Schuckman raises her head and opens her eyes. Judi Avener steps off the mat. Karen stares down at the wooden horse for a long moment, her eyes vaguely frightened, and then, suddenly, she is off. She races toward the horse with long, lengthening strides, building speed as she moves, her eyes now wide with fear, her mouth open slightly and pulled back and down into her jaw as if by the force of gravity. When she reaches her coach she leaps into the air—aided in flight by her coach's supporting hands on the small of her back—and performs a not quite perfect somersault about five feet above the horse, landing on the padded mat on the other side. Her heels touch with such force that even a bystander can feel the shock traveling up his spine.

Once she leaves the gymnastics room, dressed in rumpled corduroy slacks and a Capezio t-shirt, Karen

Schuckman seems actually to have diminished in size from the girl in purple tights who is a bit too big for gymnastics. She seems to have grown slack, to have lost her tenseness, all the steely drawing up of her mental and physical resources that is so evident when she is performing her routines. Karen walks about the Penn State campus with a deferential slouch, eyes downcast, as if, by not seeing, she can become invisible. She seems, in a sport demanding "an *extremely* strong ego," according to her coach, to be completely lacking in self-confidence. She brushes off her successes at Penn State as if embarrassed by mention of them.

"I don't think gymnastics is very healthy for your body," says Karen Schuckman after practice. "It puts all kinds of unnatural stresses and strains on you. My back's been bothering me lately. But when you turn upside down like that you get this terrific body rush of adrenaline and blood. It's a physical high. That's the first thing I remember as a child. I used to love the feeling I got when I stood on my head or hung upside down from a tree limb or did cartwheels. It felt so good. The mental part comes later. The satisfaction from beating someone and stuff. That's when it starts to screw you up."

At the age of thirteen Karen's love of "hanging up-side down" had brought her to a point where she was competing successfully on a national level and was on the threshold of a berth on the U.S. Olympic team. Her days and nights were filled with gymnastics. She practiced two hours each morning, and then, after school, traveled for an hour on the Connecticut Thruway (she grew up in tiny Bethlehem, Connecticut) to New Haven, where she taught gymnastics to children younger than herself. "The feeling is," she says, "that by teaching others you learn why you do things." After her lessons were over, Karen practiced another two or three hours, then returned home often as late as midnight. On weekends she traveled around the country competing in various AAU events. She was the AAU Junior National Champion when she was in ninth grade.

Of her grueling schedule Karen says, "I don't think it was very conducive to the psychological health of a thirteen-year-old. It would have been pretty hard on anyone, much less a young girl. I was always worn out physically. My parents didn't think it was very healthy for me. The atmosphere, that is. I was staying overnight during the weekends. I started to party, to develop a social routine outside of the gym but which included mostly gymnastics people. There were a lot of far-out people in the sport. They were mostly older. People I had strong feelings for were ten years older than me. My first boyfriend was twenty-three—I was fifteen. People worried about the sexual aspect of that kind of life. I don't know. I looked at my friends in school and saw what they were doing at fifteen and realized what a really *warped* social life *I* had. But I don't know whether it was good or bad. It's what you learn from it that's important. More important than the experience.

As a young kid you don't understand what's happening, how you got there, the route you took. You know only that you started to do it because it was fun and then you had a guide who led you and you never thought about it. You just followed." Like most young girls who are Olympic-caliber athletes, Karen first discovered the extent of her talent as a pre-teenager. An adult coach said her talent had possibilities beyond her imagination. And because those possibilities were beyond her imagination, the only way they could be fulfilled was if Karen surrendered, unquestioningly, into that coach's hands. When Karen acquiesced, at the age of ten, her two successive coaches became the most dominant force in her life for the next six years. Such relationships between young girls and their coaches are common in Olympic circles and usually result in the athlete developing an emotional dependence on her coach that transcends her sport. If that coach is a man, as was the case of Anne Henning, the Olympic speed skater, he becomes "like a father to me." Or, as in the case of others, he becomes a romantic figure.

Karen Schuckman's first coach, or guide, was Muriel Davis Grossfeld, one of the nation's foremost gymnastic coaches and a member of the President's Council on Physical Fitness. Ms. Grossfeld, who coaches at Southern Connecticut State College, has a reputation for being a severe taskmaster, unlike Karen's present coach, Judi Avener. Judi says of Ms. Grossfeld, "It's not uncommon for girls to cry hysterically during one of Muriel's sessions." Karen refuses to talk about her years under Ms. Grossfeld's tutelage other than to say, "She has all kinds of reputations and I don't want to contribute to them either way. She's great at getting the best out of you. She derives a great satisfaction from coaching, only I'm not sure where that satisfaction really derives from."

As a pre-teen and young teenager, Karen found it pleasant to surrender the distracting and minor details of her daily life to Ms. Grossfeld's custodianship, but as she matured and grew more assertive, conflicts arose. "Muriel is a very dominating person," says Karen in an unguarded moment. "She wants to be the controlling force in your life. She didn't like it when I started having friends outside of the sport. Then I started to question what I was doing." Karen's estrangement with Ms. Grossfeld grew, and she became disenchanted with her Olympic quest. During the 1972 Olympic trials she was emotionally drained and was suffering from a painfully hurt back, yet still was on the threshold of becoming at least an Olympic alternate. However, her more independent lifestyle had aroused the disfavor of what she calls "important political figures in gymnastics."

"They didn't like the image I was projecting. Neither did my parents. I was told that if I reformed my image I might make the team. By then I just wanted to go home and forget the whole thing. It had been so much fun at first. But now, at practices, I was no longer thinking about what a good time I was having, but of what I had to do to become an Olympian. I was sixteen at the time I quit gymnastics."

Karen enrolled at Penn State two years later without a scholarship and with only a vague intention of returning to gymnastics. In fact, one of the reasons she enrolled at Penn State was because, as she puts it, "Their women's team was crummy." She decided to begin competing again in her freshman year when it became apparent that there would be a great deal less pressure on her than when she had been an Olympic aspirant. "I'd thought a lot about what had happened to me over the summer," she says, "and I finally got things together. I love gymnastics and I was so glad to get another chance. It gave me the opportunity to be self-motivated, to start my career all over again when I'm much less likely to be led astray. College is really such a good place for me. I'm thinking about things now. It's really fun to be able to do something your body's good at and which gives people a lot of enjoyment to watch. It *would* be nice to have the same quality of gymnastics in college as before, but without that Olympic atmosphere. Muriel used to laugh at college gymnastics. But I'm no longer interested in it as a competitive thing. It's more aesthetic with me now. I want to get into professional dancing. For example, I'm working with a group of musicians who develop the music for my free-x routines. I think the music is as important as my gymnastics —they should enhance one another. It's really great if people can listen to a really far-out piece of music and enjoy it just as much as they enjoy watching me.

"I've got my own plans for my life, and it's good that Judi understands that. We meet on an equal level now. There's no pressure at Penn State to produce a national championship or anything like that. The feeling among the girls is that scholarships give the girls a chance to compete and to go to school for free. I'm not really involved in women's sports here. My attitude sort of divorces me from it. But I've had a lot to do with upgrading women's sports at Penn State because I'm the first woman to stand out as an athlete. I get equal publicity and recognition with any athlete here. They've used me, too. They made me an All-American here, the first time ever for a girl. I'm changing things just by being what I am."

FIGHT, LADIES!

In Lock Haven, Pennsylvania, on Saturday morning everyone eats the big breakfast: an Egg McMuffin at McDonald's. One chill, misty morning last fall when the citizens of this tiny Pennsylvania town arrived before 8 A.M., as was their custom, they found the lines at McDonald's stacked with dozens of young women all similarly dressed. They wore white blouses with Peter Pan collars, variously colored plaid kilts, and Adidas soccer shoes with plastic cleats that clattered against the tile floor like a thousand castanets. Waiting in line, the girls chatted with great animation while leaning on their field-hockey sticks. They represented state colleges that had come to Lock Haven to compete in the Lock Haven College Invitational Field Hockey Tournament, whose first game of the morning would begin at 8:30 A.M. Each team would play five games throughout the day. The games are separated by thirty-minute breaks and an hour lunchtime, during which the girls in clusters of three and four, their hockey sticks over their shoulders like rifles, walk three-quarters of a mile back to McDonald's for lunch and then back to the playing field.

The hockey field, like the town itself, is carved out of the surrounding mountains. It is a plateau walled in on three sides by rising shelves of jagged rock. Hovering like a lid over the field early in the morning is a low-lying mist, which darkens the field. From the sidelines the girls appear as tiny black shadows moving against the dark backdrop of the rising mountains. It is not until later in the morning, when shafts of sunlight break through the mist and fan out across the field, that the girls are illuminated clearly, if only for a fleeting moment, as they race through the shafts of light in pursuit of the wooden hockey ball.

The games are played in an eerie half-silence punctuated by the clack-clack-clack of stick against stick as two opposing girls fight to dig the ball out of the corner of the field. The girls grunt and sweat, jostling one another amid warnings, "Keep your stick down, please!" Finally, with an echoing whack, one girl propels the ball downfield. There is a sudden pounding of feet as both teams thunder after it, converging like a stamped-ing herd on the solitary goalie, gnomelike in her pads and waiting small and defenseless in the net. The racing girls' legs churn furiously like those of bicyclists, their short skirts flouncing with a dancer's rhythm. And yet, curiously, their upper bodies are held stiff, almost regal, heads up. They breath out heavily in small puffs of mist that blow before them.

As the girls race downfield they are watched along one sideline by a few dozen spectators, mostly opposing players sprawled on blankets, sipping from cups of steaming coffee that they cradle, prayerfully, in both hands. Occasionally someone cheers the action, "Nicely cut, Peggy, nicely cut!" The cheers are indiscriminate and rarely directed at any one team, but usually at a well-executed maneuver by an individual player re-gardless of school. In fact, the purpose of this tourna-ment is not to produce a champion but rather a show-case in which to pick the best players for an all-star team.

The most partial observers at each game are the coaches, like Gillian Rattray, the English-born coach of the Penn State team. Miss Rattray, a tanned, trim woman in her forties with a younger woman's blue eyes, is dressed neatly in a pants suit. She follows the action along the sidelines walking casually after her racing girls with her arms folded across her chest as if merely taking a stroll through her native countryside. She always trails the action. Occasionally she calls out an exhortation—"Fight, ladies, fight!"—in an offhand, barely raised tone of voice (she does not have to shout since her distinctive accent is easily discernible on the field) that carries no sense of urgency or admonishment. Her words are those of a faintly miffed schoolmistress who, although having some interest, still seems to view the proceedings, her girls, their efforts and life in general with a certain ironic detachment.

It was Miss Rattray, for instance, who suggested that her girls walk to McDonald's for lunch after they had finished their third game of the morning. "The exercise will be good for them," she said, with only a faint grin. "It'll keep them from getting stiff before the afternoon games." The girls accepted her rationale without complaint and took off for McDonald's cheerfully. Unlike most men in varsity sports, it seems women do not expect special considerations such as team meals. Nor do their coaches. One night, for instance, she was eating dinner in a well-known restaurant off the Penn State campus when a waiter approached her table, cleared his throat a few times, looking embarrassed, and then informed her that Joe Paterno had just entered the restaurant. "Isn't that nice?" said Miss Rattray, and returned to her meal.

"You don't understand," the waiter said. "He's the football coach. This is his table."

"Well, aren't we lucky then, sitting at his table."
"He always eats dinner at this table," added the waiter. "Would you please move to another table?" Miss Rattray smiled at the waiter's joke. "You *are* kidding!" she informed him, and returned to her dinner. It was only when the waiter persisted that Miss Rattray and her companion found it necessary to inform him only half in jest that she was the field hockey coach, a position that certainly took precedence over that of a mere football coach. Finally the waiter retreated. Recalling that moment, Miss Rattray smiles and, without rancor, says, *"Can* you imagine? Isn't that a scream?" Pausing, she adds, "Poor Joe."

One of Miss Rattray's star performers in that Lock Haven tournament was Barbara Doran, a twenty-one-year-old senior halfback from Swarthmore, Pennsylvania, who would eventually be picked to the Mideast All-Star team. Barbara is one of three seniors on the field hockey team to be given athletic scholarships in their final year, the first such scholarships in the school's history. She also plays on the lacrosse team, a sport she describes in aesthetic terms—"constantly flowing, airborne, a beautiful sport." She once played on the Penn State basketball team, but abandoned the team because she felt it wasn't being run on a serious level and also because of "personality clashes."

Barbara Doran, perfectly at ease, sits Indian-style on a sofa in a motel room in Lock Haven. She is about 5′ 5″ tall and weighs 128 pounds. She has an appealing figure that tends more toward the hourglass popular during the 1950s rather than the pencil so prominent today, which might explain why she is dressed in a bulky crewneck sweater, baggy carpenter's overalls and laborer's orange shoes. Her face, like her figure, is pretty in a 1950s way—large brown eyes, upturned nose, open (not cool or detached) smile and, generally, the kind of soft, undistinctive good looks one remembers in Annette Funicello, Connie Francis and a thousand all-American cheerleaders, which is what Barbara was in high school.

"I'm very competitive," she says. "I have a very strong ego and in high school the most competitive field open to girls was the cheerleading squad. I was the captain. I went steady with the football hero. God, how I hated that image! Yet, he was a nice guy. *Really*, he was!"

Although her voice softens and she seems to blush, Barbara Doran further claims that she is "a very aggressive woman." As proof she cites her continued harassment, since freshman year, of the Penn State athletic department and the school newspaper for its inadequate coverage, recognition and opportunities for women in sport. It is a cause she first espoused in high school. She makes that admission about her nature grudgingly, with more confusion than pride, as a person tends to admit something he or she never noticed, never cultivated, but is forced to admit in the face of overwhelming external opinion.

"I was more prominent as a cheerleader in high

school than as an athlete," she says. "In the afternoon I'd play field hockey or basketball before practically no one and then rush home, put on my makeup and go cheer for the boys' teams before big crowds. I started to complain to the athletic department about lack of publicity for the girls in the papers and the fact that we had no real tournaments open to us. The boys' teams had all the opportunities. I'd say to my coach, Miss Peck, a very demanding, aggressive and self-assertive woman, 'Why can't we have this or that?' and she'd just say, 'We're not allowed to, that's all.' That really surprised me. Women high school coaches are all so fierce with us, and yet they still accepted second-rate status from the school administration. Mostly my coaches were single women, and although they were assertive with us I don't know whether they could be the same when confronting men administrators. It's kinda sad, I think.

"Anyway, in my senior year we finally got the opportunity to go to Europe for three weeks on a field-hockey tour. That's when I had my first fight with my boyfriend. Would you believe he had the guts to say we didn't deserve to go, that the football players should go instead, because they're the ones who went out and sweated. That just burned me, the idea that girls don't or maybe shouldn't sweat in sports. You know, referring to a sport as 'a woman's sport' because you don't sweat too much. We do tend to emphasize skill, finesse and grace rather than brute strength, though. Lacrosse, for example, is a very graceful, skillful game as played by women and nothing like the more physical lacrosse that men play.

"Anyway, I got this reputation in high school. One time I went with this boy and at the end of the night he said I was so different than he'd expected. 'I thought you'd be such a tomboy,' he said. 'You play sports and all, and you cut your hair short.' I just wanted to cry. That was so different from *my* self-image. I mean, *I* got my hair cut short to imitate Barbara Feldon! I figured things would change when I got to Penn State, liberal attitudes and all. None of that outside bull here. But after a few months I realized it wasn't my idea of what college sports should be for women, and I went on a rampage against the school newspaper. I'm a journalism major so I started by sending letters to the sports editor asking why there were nine varsity women's sports and no coverage of them in the paper. None of my letters got published, so I finally went down there looking for the editor. I made sure I was, you know, very sweet, 'Oh, is the sports editor here by any chance?' And there he was, this little rat hunched over a typewriter. It was all very nice and cordial, we didn't want to antagonize one another. He said there wasn't enough interest in women's sports, and besides he only had five guys on the staff and no women reporters. I said, 'Why not put a guy on women's sports?' He looked at me and I'll never forget what he said: 'We have our ego, you know!'

"Well, finally I got a letter published by having a male friend of mine sign his name. By then I was getting so obsessed with the whole thing I forgot what my purpose was. I took out an ad in the paper—I paid for it—thanking the sports staff for their inspiring in-depth coverage of the Lady Lion's lacrosse team, referring to two four-line stories that were the only ones to appear all season long. They offered to do an article on women's sports if I'd withdraw my ad. You know, shut my mouth. I refused."

Barbara admits that the situation for women athletes at Penn State has changed considerably since her freshman year. They now have full coverage in the newspaper and, like male athletes, they are being given scholarships in some sports, although certainly not as many as for the men. Yet, despite her campaign in behalf of women's sports, Barbara Doran does not want the women's programs to be run on the same level as the men's. She hopes scholarships will not bring with them the attendant pressures to win championships and titles. She wants only that women be rewarded with the same recognition and the same opportunities as men to compete on an organized, proficient level in sport. It seems, after all, that she is not the aggressive person she believes she is, or rather was led to believe. What she confuses as aggression in herself is merely a healthy and highly developed sense of self. Ego. Aggression, such as Bobby Fischer's desire to crush an opponent's ego, finds its fulfillment in another's destruction, while a strong ego demands only recognition in its own right, at the expense of no one else. For example, in a questionnaire Barbara filled out for the athletic department, she was asked "Who has been your primary inspiration in athletics?" Her reply was, "Me, that's who it comes down to."

"Philosophy like Bobby Fischer's may be why we've survived through the centuries," she says, "but it's not why women play sports. Really, we play for the love of the game, not to act out aggression against someone. I never start a game thinking about winning or losing. I don't care if we win or lose, only if we play well. My attitude will never change. It may sound corny, but I believe women have been right all these years. Sports *is* for 'personal human growth.' A mature person tries to find the intrinsic value in a thing, and isn't motivated by externals. The whole athlete thing for me is a way of being, an attitude toward myself."

REPOSTÉ!

The fencer, a gangling girl, lunges wildly at her smaller opponent. The opponent leans away from the thrust and parries with a disdainful backhanded flick of her foil. She rips off her cagelike mask and jams it under her armpit. "I will not have that," she says in measured tones. "Do you understand? I will not have my girls fencing that way." She speaks without anger, a woman who finds comfort in neatly trimmed edges and so clips off the final letter of every word with a single, precise snip of her voice. The girl lowers her head, nods. She does not bother to take off her mask. She is wearing a white quilted chest protector with long sleeves, black leotards and fencer's sneakers. Her opponent is Mrs. Beth Cramer, the coach of Penn State women's fencing team.

Mrs. Cramer, in her late twenties, is wearing a beige chest protector over a turtleneck sweater and navy ski pants. She is a short, rigidly upright woman, very attractive in that Town and Country-Hunt Club way: no makeup, trim, athletic-looking and sturdy, very sturdy, but not unbending. She taps her foil on the floor and says, less sternly but still with a firm voice, "I am serious now. If you persist I will not fence you in a match." She pulls her mask from under her arm and in the same motion flips it over her face and assumes her stance. Practice continues.

Watching from the sidelines, Lisa Geisler, a twenty-year-old political science major and the women's No. 1 fencer, says, "No one calls her Beth. It's Mrs. Cramer. She's very severe, very proper. When the team goes away to fence we have to dress accordingly. We must represent the school in a dignified manner, she says. Once at an airport a group of people asked us if we were from a convent." While talking, Lisa Geisler is poised in that aristocratic, almost haughty stance of a fencer. Her mask is tucked under one arm while the other arm is extended away from her body, the hand limp as if about to be kissed. In it she holds her foil, like a brittle cane, its tip balanced lightly on the floor. Her feet are curiously parted. Her left foot points forward, like a model's, while her right foot points to her right, as if she were preparing to walk both north and east at the same time. ("A fencer's stance," she says, "you can always tell a fencer. It's a strain on the legs at first, but you get used to it.")

Like the others, she is wearing a white chest protector, basketball shorts and striped sweat socks. She is a well-built girl, 5'6" and 130 pounds, with exceptionally strong-looking legs. "Mrs. Cramer won't fence us if we don't have a good style," she continues. "Even if we can win in a match, she still won't put us out there if we'll embarrass her. That's what first attracted me to fencing —the style, and the strategy. There's nothing instinctive about it. Those who fence on instinct can do only so well, and after that their instincts won't do what quick thinking will. Smarter people, who think fast, make the best fencers. One of our fencers is a Classics major. (Lisa Geisler is going to be a lawyer. "Fencing in a courtroom," she says. She has a scholastic average of 3.88 out of a possible 4.0.)

"The Cornell team," she continues, "is very classy, very sophisticated. Of course, some fencers are prima donnas, too. They look very arrogant when they come out on the strip. The strip is called the pisté. It's actually just a long rubber mat about six feet wide and forty feet long. You have to stay on the mat when fencing, so that limits your movements basically to just two—forward and backward. If you step off the mat you lose points. Fencing is all very controlled. Sometimes, though, I'd like to go into an empty room with my opponent and just have it out like Errol Flynn.

"To some extent there is a blood-and-death attraction to the sport even if the foils are tipped and electrified. Mrs. Cramer makes us control that feeling, however. We're not allowed to cheer when we score a point, or cry out at a thrust, or even cry if we lose a match. We have to shake hands with our opponents after every match. We keep everything contained. Sometimes, though, I'll be struck by an opponent and *she'll* cry out, 'Et! là!' And I wonder if at that moment she really wasn't thinking, 'Kill!'

"I have trouble with wild opponents. They tend to draw me out. Mrs. Cramer teaches us to stay small, controlled. The men fencers at Penn State are not as controlled as we are. They use their strength and speed more, project it into the foil. They try to dominate physically. They're wilder than us, they come onto the strip with a different attitude than women do. We look at fencing as a sport, as a matter of style, a way of improving ourselves. They look at it as something to win, to dominate, and the best way to win when first starting out is to hack away. Mrs. Cramer says they'd prefer to win even at a loss of style. For us, style comes first. It's not really a man-woman thing. It's more a competition of styles. Although our style is found more with women, it's also the style of the French Masters. I worked with such a Master and he taught me all these fine moves and controlled finger work. Really, the better men fencers fence that way. That's why I wouldn't like to see the men's and women's teams integrated. I like our style better. We only fence the men for practice. We can normally hold our own against them.

"They don't get scholarships and neither do we. They didn't want them. Neither does Mrs. Cramer. She worries that scholarships will cause friction between the girls. That's also why she never lets us fence among ourselves. If we start competing among ourselves we might not get along. I know a few girls who would like to knock me off, and I'd like the chance to put them in their place. We're all very individually oriented. Once we tried to do an activity as a team and we were tripping all over one another. It was really funny. We talked about it after and decided we could only do individual sports, like fencing. It's doubly rewarding. You can win as an individual and as a team. Anyway, as to scholarships, I think it's important to give them to people who need them. As for myself, I'm here to study, not to fence. I didn't fence before I came here and I probably won't be fencing after I leave. There really aren't that many opportunities for fencers unless you live near big cities, like Philly. Besides, if I wanted to continue, say, to make the Olympic team, I'd have to give up everything else for four or five years—a fencer doesn't reach his peak, usually, until thirty—and I'm not willing to do that. It's not worth it, in my opinion, not even for the recognition. My life outside of fencing means more to me. It's like when I was kayaking—I'm also on the canoe team here—and the coach tried to get me into that syndrome. He told me if I put all my time into it I could make the U.S. team for the World Games. As it was I was working out three hours a day! I originally got into kayaking in high school because it was one of the few sports open to girls, and even at that I had a difficult time with the coach. He didn't want me or any girls on the team until we started winning, and then he saw it was an advantage as far as the team points went. I didn't care what he thought as long as I could compete. It's a very exciting sport. I loved running the rapids. There's an element of danger in it that first discourages you and then that's what makes you want to do it."

When Mrs. Cramer finishes her lesson with the girl in leotards she summons Lisa Geisler to the pisté. Lisa flips on her mask, which is made of tightly knit wire mesh, like a screen, and then assumes her stance. Her left foot is pointed toward Mrs. Cramer while her right foot points to the right. Her knees are slightly bent, as if she was half-contemplating sitting down. Her left arm is extended behind her at shoulder level. It is bent at the elbow so that the forearm is directed toward the back of her head, where her limp-wristed hand almost touches the base of her neck. Her right arm is extended directly in front of her, holding her foil. It is aimed at Mrs. Cramer, who is in an identical pose. The foils cross before their eyes, are still a moment. Then there is the quick click of steel as they commence. They move slowly at first, feeling each other out, their foil tips making little circles in the air, then darting forward a bit, parried with a click, retreating, making circles again, until finally Lisa takes the offensive.

She advances on the retreating Mrs. Cramer amid the sounds of slashed air and clicking steel and the rhythmic *pa-ti-ta-ta-ta-TAT* of feet slapping the mat. The final *TAT* comes on a strong lunge that causes the muscles in Lisa's thighs to quiver and propels her blade directly at Mrs. Cramer's chest. Mrs. Cramer parries— "Good!" she says—and makes her reposté. Now it is Lisa who is retreating and Mrs. Cramer who is advancing. And then, shortly, their roles are reversed again, and again as they continue to draw one another backwards then forwards on the pisté as if their foils were magnetized and every thrust drew from the other a harmonious parry, or as if both were merely puppets drawn by the same hand in a meticulously choreographed ballet amid the slashing of air, the clicking of steel and the rhythmic slapping of their feet.

BIG GLO

Big Glo is pacing herself. It is only the second week of basketball practice and she does not want to peak too soon. "I'm testing, mostly," she says. "The freshmen." Last year as a junior, Gloria Moyher, a twenty-one-year-old forward from Latrobe, Pennsylvania, played regularly on Penn State's scholarship-free women's varsity basketball team. This season, with the arrival of three talented freshmen, all of whom received athletic scholarships, Gloria finds herself relegated to the bench. "Sixth man, maybe seventh," she says. "And I don't like it."

Before practice begins each afternoon at White gymnasium, Gloria dribbles off to an unoccupied corner basket and practices alone. She is wearing low-cut white sneakers, high striped sweat socks, red shorts and a blue t-shirt with "U.S. Marine Corps" stenciled across the front. She is big, solidly built, but without the well-defined musculature of a man. She stands almost 5'10" tall and weighs 150 pounds. She delivers such information without a blush or a pause, as any athlete would. And unlike many tall women, she neither stands nor moves with a slouch. In fact, she carries herself so rigidly upright that she seems actually to be straining for additional height.

Her practice routine seldom varies. She stands at the foul line with her back to the basket. She pauses a second to think, then fakes left and dribbles right. She stops ten feet from the basket and pulls up for a jump shot. Her feet barely leave the court. She pushes the ball off the heel of her palm rather than flicking it off her fingertips. The ball rotates slowly in an extremely high arc before it falls straight down, swish, through the basket. During intersquad scrimmages she moves cautiously. Lumbering is the word that best describes her movement. She cannot instantaneously halt or alter the direction of her momentum, but can do so only through a dogged effort, head lowered, forcing herself to stop on the ball of her forward foot as if stepping on a cigarette butt before she can cut to the right.

Possibly her slowness stems from the fact that she seems to be thinking a great deal on the court rather than just cutting and driving on instinct as does Pat Daley, a freshman on scholarship. Daley is tall and spindly, with pigtails that stick out comically from the sides of her head. She does not look much like an athlete, certainly not as much as Gloria does, and yet in high school she competed extensively in interscholastic high-jumping, cross-country running and basketball. Scrimmaging now, she is in perpetual motion, driving toward the hoop, feeding off, rebounding, penetrating, always forcing the action, generating momentum without thinking.

"She's hustling a lot more than I am," says Gloria, adding that her apparent lack of hustle is just a conscious effort. "I'm just biding my time."

Gloria comes to life only briefly during the scrimmage. At one point she finds herself at the foul line, her back to the basket, a smaller opponent guarding her. She calls out for the ball, gets it, pauses an imperceptible split second, fakes left, drives right, pulls up, swish.

At twenty-one, with her athletic career about to come to a close, Gloria Moyher finds herself a modestly talented athlete who, given different circumstances, might have become very good (never great, however, since she moves too slowly and deliberately with none of a great athlete's instinctive reactions). Still, she is not what she could have been. At one time, as a young girl, she competed equally with boys her own age. She was welcomed in their games because, as one boy put it, "You can play as well as any of us."

"I played sports in a casual way," she says. "I never thought of training year-round for any one sport. I played football in the fall, basketball in the winter, baseball and swimming in the summer. I just followed the cycle like any young kid does."

When she reached her teens, Gloria found that while the boys her age were being encouraged to go on in sports to a highly competitive level, she, like most girls, was being discouraged from competing at the same level. She was discouraged by such comments as, "You're fourteen and you still play football!" and by the fact that her high school had no interscholastic athletic program for girls. Without such competition, her athletic talent which, up to then, had kept pace with that of boys her own age, began to fall behind.

"I always seem to be on the fringes of things," she says today. "After I graduated from high school they began a girls' interscholastic athletic program. When I first came to Penn State there wasn't much emphasis on women's sports. The philosophy then was, women compete in sport for sport's sake. You know, to have fun, to make friends and at all times to be a lady. 'Oh, excuse me for stepping on your foot, dear!' That kind of thing. Now that I'm about to graduate, they're giving athletic scholarships and the thinking is, women *can* compete on a highly skilled level. Certainly we can't be as skilled as men but we can achieve a certain degree of proficiency compatible to our bodies. Success in men's sports is supposed to be measured by the degree of skill *they* achieve. Actually, I think it's measured by gate receipts. That's one of the hassles women are going to have to avoid now. For example, our basketball team is playing in the Steel Bowl tournament prior to the men's games. They're just using us as a gimmick to get people in to see the men play.

"I think scholarships for women athletes are good as long as their purpose is to give someone an opportunity to go to school who couldn't ordinarily afford it. I don't think of them as being used to buy talent to make money for the school. Anyway, it's too late for me. I'll be graduated soon. I'll be commissioned a second lieutenant in the Marine Corps. I've always been drawn to the military. A woman isn't always being tested there like she is in the civilian world. You know, first be a secretary before you can do anything important. As a woman in the Marine Corps I'll get equal pay and equal responsibility. I'll even have men under my command. Perhaps I'm trying to prove I can make it in a predominantly men's world. I don't know. I do know that I would like to start a highly competitive sport's program for women in the Marines. Comparable to the men's Olympic program. It's inevitable that women get around to that."

THE SHOOTER

Sherri Landes, the shooter, is sprawled on her stomach on the concrete floor of the rifle range. She has not moved a muscle in eight seconds. Her legs are spread out behind her in an inverted V. Her spine is arched backward so that it lifts her chest about eight inches off the floor. She supports herself in this slightly painful pose by propping her elbows on the floor. Embraced in her arms, fondled with surprising tenderness, is a .22-caliber rifle. Her head is inclined toward her right so that her cheek presses against the rifle's wooden stock. Imperceptibly she snuggles her cheek more firmly against the stock until she can feel, under the flutter of her lashes, the rifle's metal barrel. She pinches her left eye shut and focuses her right eye through the barrel's sight toward a target fifty yards away.

The target, a bull's-eye on a square of paper the size of a napkin, is suspended from a wire by a clothespin. It looms so large and fuzzy in her sight that she cannot see its outer circles, only two inner circles and the bull's-eye itself, a spot the size of a bottle cap. Still staring through the sight, she reaches up with her right hand and, with a delicate screwing motion of her thumb and forefinger, adjusts the sight. The circles constrict before her eye, grow tighter and sharper, while the spot shrinks to a clean dark dot the size of a match head. Unseen in her sight behind the target is a mound of sand.

Twelve seconds have passed and still the shooter has not so much as twitched. She can hold this still pose so perfectly because she is wearing a leather jacket, a shooter's jacket, which is so tightly fitted she can buckle it only by sucking in her stomach until it hurts. Like a straitjacket, it restricts almost every movement save one—when she raises her arms into a firing position the oddly fitted jacket locks her arms in place, actually supports the rifle so that she can hold it perfectly still for as long as a minute without being wearied by its sixteen-pound weight.

Her hair is pinned in a bun and her ears are covered by plastic earmuffs that resemble an aviator's headset. She is oblivious to the faintest sound, her own breathing, everything save the tiny dot in the center of her sight. After fifteen seconds she stops breathing. She does not draw a breath for eight more seconds, is not even conscious of not breathing, until finally she fires.

She does not hear the rifle's loud echoing "pop," nor the sound of the ejected shell casing as it tinkles, like bits of glass, on the concrete. Nor does she see the spray of sand kicked up behind the target, nor smell the burnt sulphur. She is conscious only of the tiny pin prick that

appears one-twentieth of an inch to the right of the dot
after she squeezes the trigger. She sighs and relaxes
slightly, still holding her pose, staring at her shot.

She talks to herself in throaty whispers she cannot
hear. "Nice, girl. . . . Nice shot. . . ." She seems almost
to be whispering to someone else, an unseen companion who is very close. Still staring through the sight, she
rearranges her weight on the floor. She moves across
the concrete slithering like a snake until she settles into
a more comfortable pose. Slowly she begins to rotate
her neck and shift her shoulders inside her tight jacket.
She groans softly as she relaxes her cramped muscles,
luxuriates in the sensation of one shedding a deep, pleasurable sleep. Then she grows still again and prepares
her next shot.

After ten shots (there are ten small bull's-eyes on
each target paper) the shooter pushes a button beside
her and the target moves forward on a long wire like
wash drawn in on a clothesline. It makes a whirring
noise as it moves, and when it reaches her it jars to a
halt. She picks the target from the wire and examines
it with utmost concentration. She sighs again, says to
herself, "Aw, come on, girl," and stands up. She takes
off her earmuffs and for the first time becomes conscious of the loud "pops" echoing around her and the
ejected shells tinkling on the concrete as the other
members of the Penn State rifle team practice in this
small, square, low-ceilinged room arranged with eight
firing ranges like a bowling alley. The other members

of the team are mostly men dressed in olive fatigue jackets.

Sherri Landes plucks the bobby pins from her hair, which falls in blonde streaks below her shoulders. She has a model's face—long, high-cheekboned, with blue, up-slanting, feline eyes. She unbuckles her jacket and lets out a whoosh of exhaled breath. "I've got to lose some weight," she says. "I'm out of shape." Wearing jeans and a sweater, she is tall and slim and long-waisted. "Do you know it cost me $30 just to have this jacket fitted right? The tailor had such trouble he swore he'd never do it again. None of the others have this kind of jacket." She gestures with her head toward her team-mates in fatigue jackets. "I've got three times more equipment than they do. I don't know, I clean out my locker and the stuff seems to grow. They mostly use the school's rifles. I have my own. It's worth $400. I keep it under my bed sometimes. I'm always cleaning it and playing with it. It's *so* pretty! I love my rifle. . . . Why?" She shrugs. "Cause I'm different, I guess. I'm not like them. They're just on the rifle team. I'm a shooter."

The following morning Sherri Lynn Landes, a nine-teen-year-old sophomore from Chalfont, Pennsylvania, has breakfast at the Nittany Lion Inn. She is dressed in a brown figured Qiana blouse and tan flared slacks with wide cuffs. Her eyelids are lightly blued and she is wearing lipstick. "It was the most natural thing in the world for me to pick up a gun," she says. "My father was a member of the Penn State high-power rifle team in 1965. When I was six years old he used to take me to all the meets and I used to shoot tin cans with a BB gun. I couldn't cock it though. I had to call some man to help me. Everyone thought I was *sooo* cute. I guess it was just a way of getting attention then. I've been a shooter ever since.

"There weren't any girls in my neighborhood, and most of the guys were shooters. I shot with them, and went swimming and played basketball with them, and did all the sports. Guys can do such neat stuff, can't they? Girls are always being told they can't do this or that, we might get hurt. I had to take *dancing* lessons for a while. With Miss Doitche! Ugh! When I got to high school I was the only girl shooter on the guys' team. It was the most natural thing in the world. My first boyfriend was a shooter until I started beating him in matches. Then he got into cars. I feel kinda bad about him, destroying a male ego and all. I don't consider myself a very feminine person, you know. I mean, when I put on my jacket and stuff I look like a guy. I act like a guy. All my life I've been around older guys at shooting meets. I never thought much about being a girl until I came to Penn State. They wouldn't give me a scholarship because they said they didn't give scholarships even to guys in riflery, so why a girl. I said, why not? They give scholarships to football players and girls can't play football, so we ought to be able to get a scholarship in other sports, even if guys can't. But I don't feel *too* bad about that 'cause last year I had the highest shooting average on both the guys' and the girls' team.

"At first I tried to get on the men's team. I think I was the only girl demanding to compete with the guys. They said no, and sent me to the girls' team. I wasn't very motivated there. I never shot with girls before. I'd consider it an insult to get beat by a girl! I've been beating guys for years. Anyway, I had a match average of 277 out of a possible 300, which I feel was about three points lower than I should have had. It was better than anybody on the guys' team, though. This year they changed the rules and now I'm shooting with the guys. They eliminated the girls' team, which means a lot of girls won't be able to shoot this year. Only one or two will make the guys' team."

(In the rifle team's first two matches of the season, Sherri Landes was the only girl allowed to compete with the men by her coach, U.S. Army Sgt. Joe Dilkes, a meek-looking, smooth-cheeked man who resembles Wally Cox floating inside too-large fatigues, and who talks about his ace shooter in hushed, awestricken tones. "She's sumthin' else," he says with a shake of his head. Sherri outpointed all the participants in her first two matches.)

"I love to shoot. I love the competition and the people, but most of all it's a personal pride thing with me," continues Sherri. "You can see yourself getting better and better as your score approaches 300, which is a perfect score. It's always *possible* to be perfect. And you can match your scores with anyone throughout the world. People think to be a great shooter you need terrific eyesight, but you don't. You really just line up that circle with the sight, that's all. However, if you're shooting outside the wind affects your shot. Usually you pick a prevailing condition, like a northeast gust or something, and you adjust your sight for that and then wait until it comes along before you fire. Some people have wind gauges that make a little whirring sound, like a tiny windmill. Mostly, though, a good shooter needs reflexes, hand-to-eye coordination. And concentration. I'll go into a fog when aiming. It's such deep concentration I won't even remember shooting the target. You're like a machine, just throwing bullets at the target, hitting bull's-eyes while totally unaware of anything around you. You don't feel any sensation. It's like you're dead. You stop breathing even, 'cause breathing will throw off your shot. Everything slows down—your heart, blood, head. Even when you're loading or adjusting sights you do it slowly, methodically, very relaxed. You get into a pattern, doing everything the same on every shot. Open the same box, adjust your sight, all in the same order. It's like you're psyched. And when you finally stop and look at the target, you say, 'My God, how did I shoot that! It's a perfect pinwheel, a perfect 10!' When you're thinking about shooting your shot you're not really concentrating. Whenever I miss I always remember exactly what I was thinking at the moment I pulled the trigger. When you hit a 10 you don't remember anything.

"My friends can always tell when I've had a bad day —you know, something upsets me. It'll show on my score. A rifle can really get on your nerves if you're not controlled. Rifle people tend to be very tolerant, easygoing, not hotheads. We just enjoy life. For example, before a meet we just lounge around and talk, mostly garbage about shooting. We don't eat, drink soda or coffee, or smoke. Nothing that'll give us energy or make us nervous. No physical activity at all. You want to drain all your energy away. Some guys swear they shoot best the day after a night of drinking. Hung over, they're completely relaxed, mentally exhausted. If a person is too physically fit he tends to muscle a rifle, which is bad. That's why girls are generally able to be better shooters than guys. You give a guy a rifle and he grabs it, holds it tight. Girls don't do that. They cradle a rifle, hold it like a baby, gently. They're a little afraid of rifles 'cause they usually don't pick them up as kids. A guy will grab a rifle to show he's a man, you know, 'Hey, gimme that gun!'

"Guys tend to choke in competition. They shoot great in practice and then just fall apart. There's unbelievable pressure in a match. I love it. I shoot better in a match than in practice. Girls generally do. Why? 'Cause we don't have anything to lose in a match. We're not supposed to win. The whole emotional makeup of girls keeps them from choking. But a guy, well, now

he's got more to lose, his ego and all. He's got to prove
he's a man when he shoots. That makes him choke.
That's why, when I shoot against guys, I like to shoot on
the edge of the competition, closest to my opponents.
If you're a girl and you look like you know what you're
doing it really freaks 'em out. It's kind of an ego thing
with me. I know they're watching and getting upset
and I just go methodically through my pattern. Boy,
beating guys really turns me on.

"When I'm going through my pattern before a shot
I tend to talk to myself. It's from shooting by myself too
much, I think I'm crackin' up. Once at a match with the
Penn State girls' team I made a bad shot and yelled out,
"Oh, shit!" They looked horrified! My language really
deteriorates during a match. It's mostly from shooting
with older guys during the summer. They're guys who
work with their hands: electricians, carpenters, masons,
crude guys, I guess. They curse a lot. I curse right back.
But I love 'em.

"Shooters are *so* individualistic. We tend to do things
we can't blame anyone else for if we mess up. We're not
high-strung like executive types—they could never be
shooters 'cause they wouldn't be able to relax. They'd
be shooting while still thinking about their jobs. The
earthy guys, they work from nine to five and that's it.
They don't take their job to the matches. Also, they
tend to work with machines, and a rifle's just a machine.
A beautiful machine! It amazes me! Everything on it is
so necessary, practical. There's nothing fancy that isn't

needed. To me, it's not a weapon you control other people with. Or something you use to kill animals. I have a Bambi complex. I could never shoot a little animal. Not many rifle shooters hunt. Skeet shooters do, and pistol shooters. But they're more rowdy than us. Pistols scare me. I don't like to touch them. They're weapons. My rifle, now, it's just like a golf club to me. It's something I use to throw bullets at a target. Whenever I pick it up I think *target*, not *kill*. Why, if someone broke into my room at night, it wouldn't even occur to me to pick up my rifle to scare him off."

A Few Uplifting Ladies

On February 8, 1976, a cold and drizzly Sunday in Los Angeles, about 200 spectators and 75 weight lifters showed up at the Los Angeles Police Academy auditorium near Chavez Ravine for a men's Southern Pacific Association AAU Power Lifting contest. The meet, which began in the morning and lasted six hours, attracted lifters of various ages, sizes and configurations. There were skinny youths in the 114-pound class who seemed to have got their tight-fitting t-shirts at a children's clothing store. There were older men, gray-haired and balding, who wore candy-striped weight lifter's trunks that resembled Gay Nineties bathing suits. There were 300-pound superheavyweights who wore Army boots and wide leather belts around ponderous stomachs and clumped about the auditorium like so many anthropomorphic redwoods. There were some body builders, too, less beefy than the lifters, more defined and only casually interested in their own lifting. They seemed more engrossed with their abdominal muscles, which they examined by picking up the hem of their t-shirt with thumb and forefinger whenever they passed a window.

There were also two women. They were appearing only in exhibition, although both, Natalie Kahn and Cyndy Groffman, had previously competed in power lifting contests against men and women. Neither looked like a weight lifter. Natalie Kahn, about 5'4" and 130 pounds, wore a lifter's suit, mascara and frosted lipstick. Cyndy Groffman, about 5'6" and 140 pounds, wore red-white-and-blue diagonally striped leotards and dangling earrings. They lifted in a parody of different men's styles. Natalie worried the weights, approaching the barbell for her dead lift as if it were a sleeping animal. She circled it, backed off, rubbed chalk on her hands, faced it squarely from about ten feet away, then hurried toward it, bent over, grabbed the bar and dead lifted 245 pounds to her waist. Cyndy was more exuberant and undisciplined. She sat on the sidelines until her name was announced and then just walked over to the barbell, grabbed it, and with a toss of her long wavy hair, yanked up 270 pounds while emitting a simultaneous "Aaaggghhh!"

Natalie Kahn and Cyndy Groffman are registered with the AAU as power lifters (the three power lifts are: dead lift, bench press, squat), as are over thirty other women in this country, more than half of whom live in

Southern California. The phenomenon of women lifting heavy weights is not new, however. For years, women body builders such as Shirley Patterson, a health club manager in North Hollywood, have used weights to mold the contours of their bodies. They learned, contrary to popular opinion, that when women lift weights they do not gain the bulk and increased muscle size that men do. Weight lifting pares away a woman's fat, strengthens and hardens her muscles, but does not greatly increase their size. The result is a tighter, leaner, more sinewy look that is called "definition." During the course of her body building, Shirley Patterson, who may be one of the strongest women in the world pound for pound, found herself lifting extremely heavy weights in her workouts for a woman 5'2", 112 pounds. Out of curiosity she entered a men's AAU power lifting contest not, as she says, "to be competitive against men, because all things being equal, we can't, women don't have the musculature, but rather to meet the challenge of myself against what I do in my workouts." In competition she was inspired to lift weights heavier than any she had lifted in private.

For years, many women competing in track have lifted weights to increase their strength. Cindy Reinhoudt, for example, a worker in a New York State mental hospital, is a discus thrower and shot-putter, who at 165 pounds may be one of the strongest women in this country. She can squat 440 pounds, bench press 225 pounds and dead lift 360 pounds, all of which would place her in the middle of an ordinary ten-man field. She is short and squarish, and looks like a weight lifter. She regularly appears in exhibitions and sometimes lifts as an extra "man" on a men's team since there are few women's meets in this country. Originally Cindy began weight lifting to improve her shot and discus throws for the 1963 Pan American Games, but she has begun to concentrate more on straight power lifting over the years at the urging of her husband, Don Reinhoudt, the world superheavyweight power lift champion. Often they work out together and lift in the same meets.

In fact, most of the more than thirty women registered as power lifters have gravitated to the sport either because of a male influence—boyfriend or husband—or as an offshoot of their competition in another sport, usually track events. Yet of the hundreds of track women lifting weights in this country, only a few compete in lifting contests.

Kathy Schmidt, the Olympic javelin thrower, is a UCLA senior who has spent the better part of her life rationalizing her size. She stands 6'1" and weighs 175 pounds and yet, until she mentions her size (usually among her first words to a stranger), one is not really aware of it. She began lifting weights about five years ago to improve her javelin throwing and now regularly lifts in the women's gym at UCLA, rather than in the men's gym. "I do it out of courtesy to the men," she says. "I would hold them up if I lifted in their weight room, which is something of an 'in' thing to do these days. But I'm more relaxed in the women's gym. I'm kind of a freak there, though. The only women who use the women's weight room are dancers, and they don't use heavy weights like at the squat rack. They don't even know what it is. When I load it up and prepare to squat maybe 260 pounds, they all stop and whisper, 'What's she gonna do?' When I put the bar on my shoulders everything goes quiet behind my back. It must blow their minds. Afterwards they say, 'Heh, that's real neat, but why do you do that?' "

Kathy refuses to compete in power lifting contests despite her exceptional strength (she can dead lift 400 pounds). Her reasons are varied. "I love to lift," she says. "I'm addicted to weights. It makes me feel good to do it. I feel healthier, stronger, and I can see my body taking a different shape. It's also a great release from aggressions. But mostly, I do it for the javelin. It's a total thing, lifting and throwing, and I can never see myself doing one without the other. My main interest is throwing, however, and if I trained only for power lifting contests it would take away from my throwing. Also, I don't think the public's ready to understand what it's all about, women power lifting. They treat it like a freak show, as if it wasn't serious. It must be frustrating for those women who take it seriously to know that."

Whether Kathy Schmidt is correct is debatable. At the LAPA meet in February the spectators took both women seriously. There was none of that "freak show" atmosphere one might expect, although John Askem, the SPA coordinator for the event, did admit that his idea for involving women in power lifting contests was only to draw fans to pay for the men's events. "It was a gimmick," he said, although the women competing did not see it that way. In fact, Natalie Kahn and Cyndy Groffman may be two of the most purely motivated women weight lifters in the country because neither of them has had much of an athletic background and still do not, other than their lifting. Both consider themselves nothing more or less than power lifters, which may in part explain why they compete. The track women, like Kathy Schmidt, who lift weights privately, get their competitive urges satisfied by their track competitions, so they do not need to branch off into other events like power lifting. Without power lifting, neither Cyndy nor Natalie would have much of an outlet for those competitive urges.

"I've always considered myself an artist, not a sportswoman," says Natalie Kahn, a twenty-five-year-old student from San Jose, California. She was sitting in the audience at the LAPA meet with her mother and grandmother waiting for her name to be announced to lift. The three women, white-haired, gray-haired and auburn-haired, sat identically, hands in laps, backs straight. "I had no interest even in girls' recreation at school," continued Natalie. "I never went through the athletic thing until I started going out with Bob Packer, who's the AAU coach for the U.S. power lifting team. I'd go to the gym with him and watch him work out, and one day I saw a track woman pick up a 135-pound barbell. 'I can do that,' I said. But I couldn't even roll it! I got curious as to how it would feel to strain like that, and so I started lifting with Bob. I lost weight. I felt good mentally and physically. At work I wasn't tired at the end of the day. When I lifted I felt good mentally, and when I didn't, I felt terribly guilty and weak. I began to set goals for myself. Now I'm the top-rated women in the 132-pound class, but I want to drop my weight to the 114-pound class while still being able to lift the same amount of weight. (160 pounds in the squat, 100 in the bench press, 245 in the dead lift). I'm very serious about my lifting. I don't want to go out there and be laughed at. It's gotten so I'm really into strength. I want to see how strong I can get. I finally found a thing I could do that I was good at. It's given me great self-confidence. In everything. The stronger I got the more things I felt I could do that had nothing to do with weight lifting. I'm going back to school to get my M.A. in art, for instance. I wouldn't be doing that if it hadn't been for weight lifting. I'm more outspoken, too. Bob says I'm getting more arrogant every day. It's true. The stronger I get the meaner I get. I'm getting really macho. Sometimes I actually feel superior."

Cyndy Groffman describes herself as a former nude manicurist and vice squad detective from Chicago who is either twenty-two or twenty-three years old. "I'm not sure," she says. "I started running away from home at twelve, and have been on my own since I was fourteen.

I've lied about my age so often, I'm not really sure how old I am." Currently living in Redondo Beach, California, Cyndy is one of that new breed of American women who seem always to be just coming from or going to another part of the country, and so, to be prepared for this constant uprooting, always carry their lives with them, jumbled inside a leather satchel tossed over the shoulder. She opened her satchel while waiting for her name to be called at the LAPA meet and rummaged about for a stick of gum. She spilled out pictures of her dogs and boyfriends, past and present. She looked at one, shrugged, and said, "You win a few, lose a few. I was married at fifteen. Oh, he was a real con man! He wiped me out. He sold my $2000 accordian—I played professionally at one time—for only $100. He sold my watch, my camera, my car, my radio, everything. He sold our wedding presents, he sold me. But I loved him." She shrugs again and stuffs the contents of her purse back into it.

"I've lived everywhere and done everything," she says, "and so I came out to the West Coast to start over again. My life was upside down when I got here, and then I had my car stolen and another car repossesed. I lost my job two weeks before Christmas; my roommate and her boyfriend ripped me off of $500; and my apartment was broken into. I guess that's the way to start something new, from scratch. I had been a tomboy when I was a kid, although I hadn't done anything in sports since I was fifteen. That's one reason I came out here, to get back into the physical life. I love sports. I was as big as a water buffalo when I got here, but after I started lifting weights I lost 65 pounds. I've only been lifting for a year and I don't think I'm anywhere near my maximum lifts yet. It's a great way of taking out your frustrations. I think of my worst enemy when I'm lifting. I don't do any lifts according to style. I just sort of psych myself up, grab it and lift. I'm the kinda person who's into whatever their mood calls for at the moment. A few nights ago I was sitting in a restaurant in Redondo Beach when some bikers came in. They said they were going to Encinada so, at three o'clock in the morning, I was on a bike heading for Encinada. We're going to bike across the country later this year. The bikers are my biggest fans. They cheer me on at all the meets. Well, almost all the meets. Not many of them came today, being where it's held and all."

The only member of *The Chosen Few M.C.* who did attend the LAPA meet with Cyndy Groffman was a 350-pound superheavyweight named "Lobo," who was even more visibly distinctive than either woman lifter. Lobo had a black goatee, and when he lifted he wore a yellow beret, dark sunglasses and an earring. The judges were at first critical of his beret and glasses, then thought it more judicious not to make an issue of it.

"I love to compete," Cyndy says. "I love to do things most women won't do. As far as strength goes, I've got it all over most women. That's why I'd rather compete against men. They're more of a challenge than most women. Right now I'm ranked No. 2 among women in the country in the 148-pound class. I can squat 175 pounds, bench press 105 pounds and dead lift 270. That's not anywhere near good enough to beat men, but I'm not really in this to beat them. A woman can't. Besides, I'm a woman. I'm not trying to lift as much as a man to show them up. I don't hate men. I love men. When I go out on a date I don't carry my barbells with me. And I dress Frederick's of Hollywood all the way. I keep my mouth shut because a man's a man, and I keep my hands to myself . . . in the beginning anyway."

Cyndy Groffman is an extra lifter on a men's team operating out of Redondo Beach. She claims that just being with the team has given her an identity she has never known. "All my life I've been on my own and this is the first time I've ever had a common interest with a group. My mother in Chicago was shocked, not by my weight lifting but by the fact that I had finally stuck to something for any length of time. More than anything in the world I want to break every woman's weight lifting mark. I want weight lifting to be the main thing in my life. It's the only thing I ever started and carried through."

Cyndy Groffman was introduced to weight lifting almost by accident. She was the only woman to show up at an exhibition by Shirley Patterson, a body builder from North Hollywood. Shirley had already lifted in a number of men's power lifting meets, and had tried to get other women interested in lifting so that she could organize women's meets. She says, "At first I thought I was the only woman lifting heavy weights in a gym, but then I realized there must be others only we don't know about one another. So I approached the SPA and asked them to start a woman's program. John Askem appointed me the women's coordinator."

A few months afterwards, on September 30, 1975, at Glendale California, the first all-women's AAU power lifting championships were held in the United States. Over thirty women competed in various weight classes, with Natalie Kahn winning her 123-pound class, Cyndy Groffman winning her 148-pound class and Shirley Patterson taking her 114-pound class in addition to being picked the overall best lifter in the meet. She was thirty-nine-years-old.

When Shirley Patterson talks to people she looks directly into their eyes. When she listens she holds the same pose, although it is broken by a constant flutter of eyelashes, quiver of lips and involuntary shakes of her head. She holds her ground only by the sheerest act of will. She has large, three-dimensional eyes, delicate bones, and a nature that suggest a tightly strung animal one twitch from flight. As a child she was strictly raised. Lonely, withdrawn and introverted, she amused herself with dolls and dancing in empty rooms and with a host of "feminine things" dominated by her dream of becoming a beauty queen. At the age of twenty she bore some resemblance to a beauty queen. At thirty that resemblance was more pronounced. And today, at the age of forty, after two marriages and two divorces, and after having raised three children single-handedly, she has the fresh face and perfectly developed body of a nineteen-year-old baton twirler at Ole Miss. Only her body is not so soft. It is more defined, devoid of that layer of fat on most women which fills in the area between muscle and bone and softens their contours. Shirley acquired this look over the last twelve years by a routine of weight lifting that would have wilted most ordinary men. As a power lifter she can dead lift 225 pounds from the floor, squat down and up again with 180 pounds on her shoulders, and bench press 125 pounds over her head. She is one of the few women in the country who can bench press a weight greater than their own body weight. Another, Rebecca Joubert, a University of Tennessee junior, recently won a men's 132-pound power lift trophy at the Chattanooga Open with a bench press of 135 pounds. Generally, though, a proficient male lifter can bench press two and three times his own body weight.

Shirley Patterson's life divides cleanly into two parts: that period before she began to lift weights and that period afterwards. She says of the former, "Much of my teenage years is a blank. I was very sheltered. My parents treated me like a possession. They would never let me do any real sports. I've always felt that, given the opportunity, I might have become an excellent gymnast." As an act of independence, she ran away to get married at eighteen, but after three children, a divorce and a second marriage, she still felt, she says, like a possession. "Both of my husbands wanted a woman who was just a wife and mother. I wanted to be more than that. I have always felt there was something missing from my life, that I had no personality of my own. I never did anything special in my youth and I had this terrible fear of getting old. I don't ever want to get old. I felt I had to do something soon or else I would be beat down. Just existing."

Shirley had always exercised at home during her first marriage, and then, during her second, she began frequenting health clubs around the L.A. area where she was introduced to weight lifting as a form of body building. Weight lifting appealed to her for a number of reasons—health, strength, looks—but mostly because it was something she could do by herself and it released the pent-up aggressions a timid woman like herself could never release in public.

She entered her first physique contest, an AAU event, at the age of thirty-six. She finished third to a nineteen-year-old and a twenty-six-year-old. Shortly afterwards she was divorced a second time. "My second husband wasn't into weight lifting," she says, "and by then I was spending a lot of time away from home. I worked as a secretary during the day, ran a few miles at the beach late in the afternoon, then went to a health club at night to lift weights. Oh, I used to have these fantastic workouts! I'd get lost in them! It may sound strange, but I made a vow not to date for a whole year, and just to devote my time to my body. Your body's the only thing you have that's your own. It gave me self-worth, a personality. It wasn't until then that I started to know myself, to really grow. It was my whole life."

Today Shirley Patterson manages the North Hollywood Health Club on Lankershim Boulevard from 9 A.M. to 8 P.M. After work she changes into her tights and leotards and goes into the men's gym to work out. "I love the men's gym," she says. "It has all those heavy-looking black weights like a gym should. The women's gym has chrome weights."

The gym is small and square. There are mirrors everywhere. Above the mirrors are photographs of body builders in different poses. The room is crowded with mats, incline boards, bench presses, squat racks, pull-up bars and, in the center of the room, an intricate-looking Universal machine. Propped against one wall are rows and rows of barbells and dumbbells and flat circular barbell plates. The plates are in various sizes and poundages, and they look like the embossed coins of the Brobdingnagians. The room is filled with massive men, lifters and body builders, all grunting and sweating and heaving under enormous weights which, when finished, they let casually drop to the floor with a clank.

Shirley, smelling of perfume, steps between these massive men. They acknowledge her with a word or two. She moves with prim yet purposeful steps, like a child through an enchanted forest, picking her way, uncowed, between towering redwoods. She goes to the bench press, slips plates on either end of the bar, lies down on the bench, grips the bar overhead and prepares to lift it. The bar and plates total 125 pounds. Shirley claims that if she concentrated on nothing else but her power lifts for a year she could eventually bench press 150 pounds. But, since she is primarily a body builder, her routine also includes many lifts that require high repetitions which are just exhausting enough to keep her from ever reaching her maximum in the three power lifts. Male power lifters are interested only in lifting their maximum weight one time, while body builders lift less than their maximum many times to pare away fat and sharpen muscle. Women, it seems, can combine both types of lifting. The heavier the weights they lift, the stronger they become and the more sharply defined their bodies; yet they still do not acquire bulk. Almost every woman power lifter in the country will admit that one reason she lifts is because lifting improves the shape of her body.

Shirley lifts the 125-pound barbell off its rack and holds it over her head. For the first time, the muscles in her arms now stand out clearly. She puckers her lips as if to blow smoke rings and then makes a series of quick breaths—"cho-cho-cho-cho"—before lowering the weight to her chest. Then, in one fluid motion, she raises it back up over her head and slips it onto the rack. She gets up and straightens the bench press a bit, as if it were a piece of household furniture she was tidying up. "I try to lift with proper form," she says. "I always want to look feminine. I don't want to go up there and grab it like an animal." She walks over to a table where she had laid out a pink notebook in which she records each day's workout. She fills in the box under bench press and then goes to the squat rack. Unable to resist, some of the men cast quick glances at her. She is wearing a wine-colored leotard cut low in front, a scarf tied around her neck, and large circular earrings that jingle when she moves. As she slips weights onto the barbell on the squat rack, she says, "A lot of what I do is for recognition. I used to skydive for a while and I made a television commercial for Jack LaLanne Health Clubs. I was thirty-six when I started skydiving. I started everything late in life. One reason I began power lifting was to get recognition for all those years in the gym by myself. I had this urge to be recognized and of course to compete. It's funny though, when I tried to recruit other women to power lift, none of the married gals was interested. They didn't feel the need to compete anymore for anything, I guess—like we single gals do. Anyway, I got that competitive phase out of my system. I don't power lift in contests anymore. I feel now that that was the wrong reason to compete, for recognition. Besides, I had begun to feel the AAU was exploiting us gals, just using us to make money for the men, money that was not going into any women's programs. I confine my lifting to my private workouts now. But I won't ever not lift. It's part of my life. I feel guilty when I miss a day."

Shirley positions herself underneath the squat rack, lifts the 170-pound barbell onto her shoulders, stands there a moment. She stares straight ahead, then says, under extreme duress, "I feel at home in a gym. In a lot of life's situations I feel uncomfortable. I'm not at ease in large groups. I go into a shell. Most of my friends are men lifters. They treat me like one of the guys and I can communicate with them in the gym in a way I can't always do outside with other people."

Shirley takes a step back now. She begans to make those quick breaths again—"cho-cho-cho-cho"—and then she squats slowly down until her rear end is almost touching the floor. She starts to rise, falters, seems unable to make it, her face contorted in pain until she lets out an anguished scream, *"Aaaggghhhh!"* and rises to her feet.

The Feminine Mystique

In Tucson, Arizona, the Orange California Lionettes upset the defending champion Raybestos Brakettes of Stratford, Connecticut, for the Women's 1969 Fast-pitch National Softball Championship and the right to represent the United States at the World Championships in Osaka, Japan, in August 1970. Before, during and after each of their two games with the Brakettes, the Lionettes played the song "The Impossible Dream." When the Lionettes arrived in Stratford on August 8 for the next year's National Championships, William S. Simpson, President of Raybestos-Manhattan Corporation, commissioned former Brakettes' pitcher Bertha Tickey to buy the record "The Impossible Dream," then ordered Dick Ondeck, the tournament announcer, to begin playing that record the moment the Brakettes defeated the Lionettes for the title. That the Brakettes, National Champions seven of the last twelve years and possibly the greatest women's softball team ever assembled, would reap their revenge on Orange was a fact as indisputable as the wetness of water. "We just have to win," said a Raybestos official. "Simpson is determined to send Orange to Japan as the second-best team in the States. And if necessary, he'll exhume Babe Didrikson Zaharias for the final game."

"Once you've tasted the championship," said Simpson, "you don't like to give it up. We've instilled a very professional attitude in the girls. The only thing they think about is winning."

The Brakettes would win, it was said, because Simpson had spared no expense in acquiring the best fans, facilities, and players in the country. The Brakettes were the only team to play their home games in an 8000-seat, lighted stadium (Raybestos Memorial Field). They were the only team who could afford to take summer trips to Florida and California for exhibition games. Their fans, who had been cultivated into rabidity by years of success, were the most knowledgeable in the country. They included older retired couples who came with their blankets and deck chairs tucked under their arms; factory workers who sat in small groups where they drank beer and "cheered the broads on"; teenage girls who walked endlessly around the park, stopping only to press their noses against the screen for a glimpse of their idols, the Brakettes; and middle-aged women in crash helmets who walked three-abreast and did not break formation for anyone.

"The Raybestos fans are the most professional I have ever seen," said Beverly Dryer, coach of the Sun City, Arizona, Saints. "They root only for good plays. Our fans root for individual girls, whether they are good or not. They sort of adopt different girls on the team, and even when we're in an important game they make me play everyone. During the year they have picnics for their favorite girls."

The Brakettes' fans do not have picnics for their favorite players, nor do the Brakettes have any players they would be afraid to play because they might lose a game. In fact, they have some of the most talented female athletes in the country, and probably two of the most talented female athletes in the world: Donna Lopiano and Joan Joyce. Lopiano, a broad-shouldered woman of twenty-three with thick, dark eyebrows that seem always to be frowning, is the most vicious pull-hitter in women's softball. She is also an excellent pitcher and alternates with Joyce between the mound and first base. Lopiano has been a first-team All-Star selection five of her last seven years, and was a second-team choice the other two years.

Joan Joyce is twenty-eight years old. She owns a travel agency in Trumbull, Connecticut, called, appropriately enough, *Joan Joyce's All-Star Travel*. She has been a first-team All-Star selection in each of her last eleven years, and was voted the tourney MVP four times. She rarely smiles. She has short reddish-brown hair, blue eyes always suspiciously narrowed, squarish shoulders and heavily-muscled legs. She moves in that twitchy, loose-limbed way good athletes do, as if perpetually limbering up for some future and, as yet, unspecified contest. Any contest. She has been an athlete all her life. She is, without doubt, the greatest woman softball pitcher in the world, who, after fifteen years, dominates her sport as no athlete, male or female, has ever dominated a sport. She once struck out 40 batters in an eighteen inning game, and in an exhibition once fanned Ted Williams. She has won over 300 games, lost less than 20, and before this tourney began was described by a male umpire as "one of the three best softball pitchers in the world. The other two are men."

Since she has dominated women's softball for years (she has been a player with the Brakettes for twelve years, ever since she turned sixteen), her continued dominance in this event will surprise few players or fans. They assume such brilliance from the Waterbury, Connecticut, native whose career, and each game in it, so nearly approaches perfection that, in a way, she is boring to watch.

"My games *are* boring," she says in a blunt voice devoid of false modesty. "To everyone but me. I set up private challenges for myself, a pitch in a certain spot, a no-hitter (she has had more than 60), a perfect game (she has had 15). Once I get a run, the game's in my hands. I can lose, but only by luck. My games must really be boring to watch. All those strikeouts. (She averages 14 per seven-inning game.) Without me in this tournament every game would be exciting."

Despite her awesome talent and near total success in softball, Joan Joyce considers herself, at 5'9", a superior basketball player (she was an All-American AAU selection in 1961 and 1965), and she prefers, above all sports, golf.

"I started playing softball at eight because my father played it and because it was the only sport open to me at the time," she says. "But I don't like it as much as I do golf. There's too great an element of luck in women's team sports. My success in softball, no matter to how slight a degree, still depends on my teammates. I play sports seriously, and not many women do. They aren't conditioned to take sports seriously or to react instinctively the way men do from their earliest years. I've always been an athlete, and as long as I play women's team sports my success won't be totally my own."

Although Joyce and Lopiano are in a class by themselves, the rest of the Brakettes are more than proficient. Most of them were either groomed on the Brakettes' minor league team, the Raybestos Robbins, or were acquired from other teams across the country. The manner in which some of these girls were acquired is what accounted for much of the bitterness felt toward the Brakettes during 1970's seven-day tournament. It was said more than once by players, coaches and even fans that the Raybestos Brakettes bought their players, and that the event really consisted of seventeen amateur teams and one professional team.

When confronted by this charge, one Raybestos fan

feigned shock and said, "Not amateurs! You must be kidding! Of course the Brakettes are an amateur team. Why don't you go to Joanie Joyce's home and ask her? And if she isn't in you can ask the servant. Of course, Simpson may be busy washing the floors, but you can wait until he finishes."

"It's bad enough that the Brakettes have such facilities they can lure girls from other teams to Stratford," said one angry coach. "But when they actively recruit our players that's downright unfair. They called my catcher five times this summer to get her to leave our club. They said they would get her an easy job, fix her up in a home and pay her way through college."

The catcher in question never went to the Brakettes, however, because as she put it, her team had just gotten new uniforms which went wonderfully with her hair. This is typical of most of the girls who competed in the event. Unlike previous years, the girls seemed as intent upon looking good as playing well. (The Sun City Saints, for example, are a youthful, exuberant team which, at times, seems composed entirely of platinum blondes running on and off the field in spotless white spikes.) Whether this attitude sprang from a sense of despair at the power of the host Brakettes, or from an evolution in the game of women's softball is not entirely clear.

"Sure we came to win," says the Saints' Ginger Kurtz, a 20-year-old platinum blonde shortstop with heavily mascaraed eyes. "But I don't want anyone forgetting I'm a girl out there."

Another player with a similar attitude is Jenny Anderson, an eighteen-year-old centerfielder from Portland, Oregon. Jenny, a freshman at Oregon State, was considered one of the most attractive players in the tourney, and the only girl to wear her long hair flowing down to her waist. During her seven days in Stratford Jenny drew a large, mostly male, following who argued continually as to whether her greatest attribute was her fine throwing arm or her even finer legs.

Early in the tournament Jenny and her equally attractive teammate, Chris Mueller, were criticized by their older Portland teammates for having only a casual attitude toward the tourney's outcome.

"The older girls wanted us to go to a pair of losers' games on the one night we weren't playing," said Jenny. "Can you imagine, on our night off! Well, Chris and I wanted to see the sights that night, and maybe meet some people since we'll probably never come East again. The older girls said if we were really dedicated to women's softball we'd go to the games where we might learn something. We could see the tournament meant a lot to them so we went. But I think a lot of these older girls are deluding themselves. They think just because the tournament means everything to them, and the clique they hang around with, that it means a lot to the rest of the world. But I don't think anyone really cares who's the best women's softball team except for that small group of people so closely involved in it that they reinforce each other's beliefs.

Some of the girls get so wrapped up in softball that they spend years in it, and instead of it being a means to an end, like meeting people and traveling and stuff, it becomes an end to them. I'm determined that won't happen to me. I'm only going to play one more year, and that only because I owe it to 'Doc.' "

"Doc" is Dr. Lawrence Bernard, the painless Portland dentist who sponsors the Oregon girls. Dr. Bernard, a droll, middle-aged quipster, is the author of his own last will and testament, which begins: "Being of sound mind and body I spent all the money on myself. . . ." He claims that he would have made an excellent stand-up comic at Grossingers if he had not forsaken his native Bronx for an Oregon dental school in 1937. There he became one of the few advertising dentists in America, which served to his advantage because, as he says, "I'm a lousy dentist but a helluva advertiser." The centerfold of the Portland press brochure features a grinning photo of the doctor alongside advertising copy that promises to quote prices in advance and to let patients sleep during extractions. Dr. Bernard claims he writes all his own copy, which includes such pearls as, "If your teeth are not becoming to you, you should be coming to us," and "Look at your teeth, everyone else does." These numerous aphorisms grace his office window, his Oldsmobile station wagon, and such assorted miscellanea as a red rubber change purse shaped like a mouth and painted with white teeth that break into a smile when the purse is pinched

open. The doctor hands these out to all potential customers.

Before Dr. Bernard took over sponsorship of the
Portland girls he had already sponsored a less proficient
group of girls called "The Salem Molarettes." When he
was about to buy their first uniforms he thought of
putting a large white molar on the back of their blouses,
but settled instead for just his name, which he felt to be
less ostentatious. He followed the same policy when he
began sponsoring the former "Erv Lind Portland Florists" in 1965. His team was called simply "Dr. Bernard's," which might be comparable to calling the New
York Yankees "George Steinbrener's." Some of the
older Portland fans, however, still refer to the team as
"Erv Lind's" or "The Florists'." Erv Lind, the former
sponsor, was a beloved softball fanatic who died in 1964
after an automobile accident in Orlando, Florida,
where he refused hospitalization rather than miss his
team's doubleheader.

When Dr. Bernard took over in 1965, the older Portland girls were annoyed with his less than reverential
attitude toward women's softball (and life in general),
which contrasted markedly with that of their former
sponsor. At first they threatened to quit en masse, but
over the years they have learned to admire the doctor
even though most of them will admit "he doesn't take
the game that seriously."

Doctor Bernard came to women's softball, he says,
because he was struck by the talent and grace of girls

playing a man's game. "I couldn't conceive of girls playing so well," he says. "The moment I saw them I knew
I had to sponsor a team. I had sponsored men's athletic
teams—softball, volleyball, basketball, etc.—but they
were always more aggravation than they were worth.
The men were too serious about their sports, too dedicated. With the girls it's different. At least it is with the
girls on our club. I've had nothing but pleasure watching them play, regardless of how well they do. Erv, the
former owner, was killed by women's softball. It was his
life. But it isn't mine. It's just my hobby. I get the most
pleasure when people tell me how good my girls look
and how feminine they are. And to be honest, I admit
that being recognized by the fans gives me pleasure,
too. Like most people, I'm an egotist. I just love to be
on stage."

This year Dr. Bernard's mostly young and inexperienced girls surprised the fans by advancing to the
finals of the losers bracket. On August 13 they met
Orange for the right to play the Brakettes, who had
marched grimly and efficiently through five games
without a loss. While the two teams warmed up, Jenny
Anderson and Chris Mueller could be seen playing
catch while twisting to the tune of "Lay a Little Lovin'
on Me," which was emanating from the loudspeaker.
Although Portland eventually lost to Orange 4–2, and
were eliminated, the Oregon girls seemed hardly
shaken by their defeat.

One of the stars for Orange that night was their left

fielder, an Anaheim schoolteacher, Maxine "Mickey" Davis. Mickey, who was born in Ware Shoals, South Carolina, is a tall, slender puff-blonde with a rich tan, the ability to blush effortlessly, and a tendency to lay her hand on the arm of any male she might be talking with. Mickey chases flyballs with delicate, quick little steps and such infectious enthusiasm that her every move brings a chorus of "Hey Mick-a-a-a-y!" from the fans.

"Oh, gosh, I hope I hit well tonight," she said prior to the Orange-Raybestos championship game. "I haven't had a particularly good season, you know. I'll tell you how bad things have been going for me," and she placed her hands flat against her lips and shook her head. "I got attacked by this man one night near my house. Really! He must have been crazy or something. Well, anyway, I broke away from him and threw my pocketbook at him. I missed! Can you imagine? And me an outfielder! There was nothing else for me to do but scream. Isn't that just like a woman? Boy, did I scream bloody murder! He got frightened and ran off. But I was so embarrassed about the pocketbook that I didn't tell anyone. Isn't that awful?"

Mickey claimed this wouldn't have happened if she had remained the local tomboy she had been as a youth in Ware Shoals. There she was considered one of "the toughest guys in town," and she often spent her time playing softball with the boys instead of dolls with the girls.

"Down South sports are a natural outlet for young girls in a small town," she said. "But we don't make a thing of it, you know, like grooming the girls for top-notch softball like they do in other parts of the country. It's just something to do for fun. I still love it, but I don't think my life is guided by it like some girls. They get so intense about it they lose all their dignity over the game. One year one of our players was beaten up by some players from another team after a game. Ever since then our coach, Shirley Topley, won't let us leave the hotel unless we're in groups of twos and threes.

"But I think things are changing now. Some of the girls used to get a little rough, I guess, because they were tired of being looked upon as fragile by men. I think that's why many of them turned to softball in the first place. They wanted men to respect them as a total person and not just a helpless object. But some went too far. They actually began to think they could compete the same as a man. I think they're crazy. Girls just aren't built the same. The only thing we have going for us when we play sports is that we can compete more gracefully than men, although not as well. Once we destroy the illusion of femininity we're defeating the whole purpose of women's sports. It's fun watching a girl compete only as long as you remember she's a girl. Once you forget that fact it becomes boring no matter how good she is. I remember the greatest compliment I ever got was when I told a man I was a softball player and he said I didn't look like one. I said, 'Thank you.'"

Because of her striking good looks, which are not unlike those of a Las Vegas showgirl, Mickey Davis was voted the tourney MBP (Most Beautiful Player) by the half-a-dozen sportswriters who sat in the Memorial Field press box for ten to fourteen hours daily. Mickey won over stiff competition from Jenny Anderson because, as one writer put it, "the way she ran, her fanny twitching like a scampering doe's, was just a shade sexier than the way Jenny tossed her hair from her eyes." This was the same reporter who, in a previous tournament, became so enamored of the sensuous way a Pekin, Illinois, pitcher released the ball that he bombarded her with literary bouquets in his daily articles. He first referred to her as "the attractive Lorene Ramsey," then as "the beautiful Lorene Ramsey" and finally, after she gave him the cold shoulder in the dugout one day, he began refering to her as "the highly overrated Lorene Ramsey . . ."

When the Lionettes took the field against the Brakettes for the first of two possible championship games, 12,000 fans were seated throughout Raybestos Memorial Stadium. Since Orange had lost earlier in the week to Stratford (Joyce pitched a no-hitter), they had to win twice tonight in order to retain their title. Most of the regular fans knew there would be only one game so they began arriving at five o'clock, and by game-time the stands were filled. As Orange pitcher Nancy Welborn completed her warm-ups, the Stratford fans were unusually quiet (partly because the game seemed such an anticlimax and partly because it was a muggy Friday evening), and for the first time in recent memory some of the regulars were missing. The most conspicuous absence was that of Nails Nish Dinihanian. Nails, a 5-6, 300-pound, cigar-chewing former slow-pitch star, had attended most of the tourney games. He always sat in the upper home plate stands where he supplied his friends with quantities of Seagrams Seven (laced sparingly with Seven-Up) and pizza pies from the Frog Pond Restaurant.

Nails had missed the Championship, however, because his house had burned down the night before. Although this was considered a valid excuse by his cohorts, still there was a faint rumbling of discontent among a few who felt that "if Nails was really dedicated to broad's softball, he woulda came."

"I don't blame Nails," said Dick Ondeck, as he prepared to announce the first Raybestos batter. "It's been a really dull tournament. Women's softball games are usually dull anyway. They're mostly pitchers' duels. But this one was particularly dull since everyone knows the Brakettes are going to win it."

After he announced the first batter, who quickly grounded out, Ondeck continued, "The only excitement in the whole seven days came last Saturday when Glen Laudenslager, our official scorer, sprained his thumb and I had to apply ice packs to it between innings. Isn't that right, Glen?"

Laudenslager, a muscular, heavily tatooed Navy veteran who had survived two kamikaze attacks in World War II, held up his ailing thumb for inspection. It was, indeed, bruised.

As the game slipped easily into the third, and then the fourth innings, Ondeck went on to admit that he, himself, had almost been a casualty of the event.

"I've been sitting here for over eighty hours, covering thirty-three games, and it's gotten so I see streaking arms and legs in my sleep," he said. "Sometimes I have the feeling I'm announcing plays that happened two outs ago, or two innings ago or even two days ago. After one extra-inning game in the middle of the week—I think it ended about 1 A.M.—I got a little hysterical. Glen tells me I started screaming, 'God, I love it, I love it, God help me, but I love every inning of it,' and then expressed a desire to be buried in the batter's box at home plate if I didn't survive the tournament."

The game had moved quickly to the seventh inning with neither team having scored. This is not unusual in women's softball, where games often go into extra innings before the hitters loosen up. Welborn, a tall, slim brunette of swanlike grace, was retiring the Raybestos hitters with a baffling assortment of off-speed pitches from an underhand motion as eternally changeless as a windmill.

What Welborn achieved by grace and deception Joyce achieved by pure and overwhelming power. She delivers the ball in an underhand slingshot motion. Her right arm snaps back toward second base and then snaps toward the plate with such force that the ball, brushing her right thigh, causes the leg to shake. Her momentum carries her far forward and to her left. She can retain her balance only by a series of short forward hops on her left foot. None of her pitches goes in a straight line. She can make them rise, sink, curve, or behave like a screwball, and she has even developed a change of pace that is equal to Welborn's. Last year Welborn had beaten Joyce twice, and this year the Brakettes, and Joyce in particular, were confident they would solve her change-up if the game went into extra innings. After seven innings the two teams were still tied at 0–0, which was a good omen for the Brakettes.

"You know these people love extra-inning games," Ondeck said, pointing to the vast crowd. "It's really crazy how devoted they are to women's softball around here. Sometimes I don't know how Glen and I keep our sanity day after day through all these games. About the only thing we have to rely on is the lemonade from Gino's Hot Dog Stand. Gino's lemonade is an excellent barometer at telling us when this tourney is just about over. In the beginning of the event Gino just dips a lemon once or twice into a glass of water before he sells it; in the middle of the tourney he just waves a lemon over a glass of water and calls it lemonade; but on the last day he thinks it's sufficient just to keep a lemon in the same room with the water to be able to call it lemonade." He raised a glass of Gino's lemonade and saluted the fans as he announced the first batter in the tenth inning.

When the fourteenth inning arrived with still no score, the Stratford fans began to stir. It should have been over by now, a fan said. The Brakettes still had not solved Welborn's change-up. If anything, they were getting more and more anxious.

In the sixteenth inning the fans began to cheer on every pitch, and in the eighteenth they began cheering not only for the Brakettes but also for Orange.

"After every scoreless inning," said Ondeck, "the Brakettes lose 200 fans to Orange."

At eleven o'clock at night in the twentieth inning, Joyce walked Orange catcher Nancy Ito. Mickey Davis singled her to third. After another walk, Welborn scored the winning run with a sacrifice fly. "My God," moaned a sportswriter in the press box. There would be a second game.

When the second game started at 11:30 P.M., amid a thick, eery mist, not more than a few hundred people had left the Stadium. They all seemed to sense that something was happening that was not in the script, and they were determined to stay to the end.

When Welborn, who pitched all twenty innings of the first game, took the mound for the second game, a great cheer went up from the fans. Donna Lopiano started for the Brakettes, who seemed to have already lost heart the moment they saw Welborn take the mound. The outcome was a forgone conclusion. In the seventh inning with the score tied 0–0, Mickey Davis doubled. She was immediately singled home by Rosie Adams, and for the second straight year, the Orange California Lionettes were National Champions.

Trophies were presented at home plate at 1:30 A.M., with Welborn winning the tourney MVP award. As the Brakettes stoically accepted their runner-up trophies, a fan shouted through the early morning silence, "They ruined the Brakettes!"

William S. Simpson, President of Raybestos-Manhattan, stood in the shadows of the Raybestos dugout, unnoticed. He looked bewildered, and every so often he would hunch his shoulders up around his neck as if to ward off a chill. "I don't understand it," he said. "We've always had the muscle when we needed it. I don't understand it."

Cha-Cha and
Her Time Machine

Shirley Muldowney is a thirty-six-year-old divorceé and mother who likes to cook, tend her lawn and decorate her ranch home in Mount Clemens, Michigan, but prefers to spend most of her time on the road chasing and sometimes catching men with nicknames like "The Snake," "The California Flash" and "Big Daddy," whom she almost caught at Indy last summer.

Like Shirley, those men were teenagers during the 1950s. They worked in gas stations and drove black '55 Chevy Nomads with the 265 c.i. power-pack option, three deuces, and two bags of sand in the trunk for traction. They were drag racers who drove in imitation of James Dean in "Rebel Without a Cause." They hunched forward over the steering wheel, listing to the left with their elbows on the door's armrest as if, like

Dean, they too were about to tumble from the car in that split second before it plunged over the cliff. Their steadies sat beside them and fiddled with the styrofoam dice dangling from the rear-view mirror. They all looked like Natalie Wood, only not so fresh-faced or full-figured. They were thin, bony girls, actually, a little scuffed around the edges, and tougher than Natalie Wood ever was. They skipped school, waitressed, talked tough and woke each morning to apply new makeup directly over the old.

Today those women are housewives and mothers and wearers of pants suits, and those men are Chrysler engineers and machine shop owners. They drive Mercedes 450 SEL's with the 6.3-liter option and an automatic transmission they always shift manually. They are still drag racers, though, only now they race on million-dollar strips, not the street. Their cars cost over $30,-000; are painted in day-glo colors; and do not even remotely resemble any '55 Chevy that ever existed or, for that matter, any other car one might expect to see in a *Big Buy* parking lot. The fastest of the men drive Top Fuel dragsters, which are long and slim like a sharpened pencil. They have a tubular aluminum frame, bicycle wheels in front and fat black slicks in the rear. In between there is an aluminum cockpit shaped like the shell of a cockroach, and behind it, a blown and injected aluminum Chrysler Hemispherical engine that cost $10,000 and never saw the light of day in any Chrysler plant but was completely fabricated by hand, cast and machined, in the private shops of men like Keith Black and Ed Pink. The engines produce almost 2000 horsepower on a blend of nitro methane fuel that propels the dragster from a standing start to a distance some 1420 feet or a quarter mile away in less than six seconds at speeds in excess of 250 mph. They can be stopped only by brakes and two sets of parachutes.

Despite such glossy trappings and yearly incomes in six figures, today's drag racers are not really much different from what they were as teenagers. Their lives, more opulent, are untouched by today's complexities. They are still dominated by a single quest, as simple and as illusive as the horizon: to eliminate time from their lives 1/100th of a second at a clip until ultimately they would eclipse time altogether in a perfect pass of 0.00 seconds.

Like those gaunt Natalie Woods of the 1950s, Shirley Muldowney became a wife and mother, too, and like those sullen James Deans, she also became a drag racer. She began racing on the city streets of her hometown of Schenectady, New York, in a 1940 Ford with a Cadillac engine, soon graduated to a potent '58 Chevy 409, and then in quick succession milked seven Corvettes dry before she hit the big-time in the National Hot Rod Association. She set an NHRA record in 1964 with a '63 Plymouth 426 wedge that eventually earned her a ride in a B/Gas dragster, the first woman ever to be licensed to drive a dragster. In 1971 she became the first woman ever to drive a fuel-burning Funny Car (essentially a

Top Fuel dragster, but heavier with a full fiberglass body). And then, in 1974, she became and still is the only woman in the world to drive a Top Fuel dragster in NHRA competition. Last spring she finished second in the Columbus, Ohio, Spring Nationals, and during the summer she finished second in the Nationals at Indianapolis to Don Garlitts, a twenty-two-year racing veteran known as "Big Daddy." Recently she became the first woman named to All-American status by the American Auto Racing Writers and Broadcasting Association. Among the only nine men to have received this honor are A. J. Foyt, Richard Petty and Mario Andretti.

Shirley Muldowney has been drag racing in NHRA competition for eighteen years. Her fans call her "Cha-Cha," a name painted in shoe polish on the side of her '40 Ford when she was a teenager. She wiped it from her car, but it has stuck to her just the same. She cannot understand why. It seems an incongruous name, with all its fiery Spanish connotations, for a thin, tightly strung and meticulous woman who seems more a youngish maiden aunt—very attractive but a bit brittle and repressed—than a drag racer. She has a long, prominently-boned face that is quite pretty in a country-and-western singer way (high cheekbones, square jaw), and the only features even faintly Spanish are her large black eyes and black hair, cut short, naturally.

She looks frail; she weighs less than 100 pounds, which is some twenty-five pounds less than her lightest male counterpart, Tommy Ivo, whom she calls "a little runt." Her lightness is both an advantage for a drag racer who figures every fifty pounds to be worth a tenth of a second, and a disadvantage for someone who must control a 1200-pound aluminum frame being propelled by 2000 horses at speeds in excess of 250 mph and under circumstances such as "tire shake," during which the tires become oblong and can literally shake a car apart. Since Shirley Muldowney does control her car under such circumstances, one assumes that she does so not with physical strength but with resolve.

"Oh, I can tell," she says, pointing to a barely noticeable discolored spot under one eye. "Most people can't, though. The doctor worked on this eye a bit and I think it looks pretty good. It doesn't bother me. I'm pretty lucky compared to some guys. There are some crispy critters in this business. For sure! I've only been burned a few times. Once at Dragway 42 a cylinder wall collapsed and my engine exploded at the end of a run. I was going over 200 mph. It was like opening a furnace door and sticking your head in. We wear asbestos fire suits, of course, and fire helmets, but still the heat was so intense it burned my eyes shut. Then in '73 at Indy my blower broke 1000 feet from the finish line. I was going about 230 mph. I knew something was wrong before it blew, but it was such a good run—you can flat tell a good run—that I just didn't want to lift my foot off the accelerator. When I finally did, the car exploded. It poured fuel all over me and set me on fire. I knew I was in a bad situation. I hit the fire bottle and then pulled my parachute, but it burned right off. I drove behind the guy in the other lane, past a guard rail into a field and came to a stop. I got out with my helmet still blazing. My eyes were burned shut again."

Even talking about such accidents, Shirley Muldowney speaks perfunctorily, as if talking to a young nephew to whom she is trying to maintain a certain decorum, the decorum of an aunt, which, she hopes, will reveal absolutely nothing about that aunt. Her talk is punctutated with calculated exaggerations—"Oh, isn't that the hot truth, though!"—always underlined by a wide-eyed expressiveness as if, like an actress, she was emoting to the last row of an audience. Every so often, however, a word will slip—"bitchin" or "motha"—that suddenly calls to mind all those James Deans and Natalie Woods and also a tough young Shirley Rocque, a French-Canadian and Indian girl who first ran away from home at the age of thirteen and lived alone for three weeks in New York City before finally returning to Schenectady.

"All I ever wanted to do," she says, "was race on the streets. I was always going 120 mph past some restaurant or racing down a hill holding hands with a passenger in a car alongside of me. Crazy stuff. The police were always on me. Oh, I wasn't a bad kid, really, not by today's standards, but I was a little, ah, chippish. Yes, chippish. I skipped school a lot. I came from a very tough neighborhood. For sure! Eventually I did graduate from high school. But I had this thing with school.

I didn't like it. I always skipped, headed for a bar. I'd stick my thumb out and the first hot rod that came by I'd get a ride. I did grow up kinda fast. I never had anything—of course, I didn't know the difference then so I didn't miss anything. My father was a teamster steward. My mother worked in a laundry for twenty-five years. I always worked, waitressed and stuff. I never had a young gal's life, not for a hot minute! I couldn't tell you what a hayride was like, that's the truth! The flat truth! I was married at sixteen to Jack Muldowney, a hard-working guy who owned a gas station and drag raced. I had a son at seventeen, and at night, when they held races up on the Depot Road, Jack and I would go racing. Of course we couldn't afford a baby-sitter, so we had to take turns baby-sitting while the other one raced. We got along great then when we didn't have anything, just two hard-working kids. I was a proofreader at a newspaper. Jack was my engine builder and mechanic when we got into more serious racing. Then, when I turned professional, it ruined his business and our lives. I was always on the road then, and so we got divorced."

Like most drag racers, Shirley Muldowney's rise to national prominence from a pursuer of two-dollar trophies to a recipient of five-figure guarantees just for appearing at a strip, was considerably less speedy than her first trip down a quarter mile in her '40 Ford. She stepped up from car to car and from class to class by lowering her ets (elapsed times) a tenth of a second and increasing her top speed by a few miles per hour each season until finally she found herself no longer driving stock-bodied cars but firmly ensconced in the more lethal dragsters. Her progress was, at first, impeded by her being a woman. When she qualified for her dragster's license at a Connecticut drag strip in 1965, the governing board of the NHRA refused to accept it. Finally forced to do so, they refused to let her race in NHRA national events, hoping that once swept under the rug, she would merely go away. "They didn't want every Emma Jean Glotz in a pink fire suit getting in a dragster," says Shirley. "But I was determined. I was just a handful for them, for sure! After three years they had to let me race. At the time I could see I was novel, that the fans loved it, but I still wasn't making any money. I began to realize that racing wasn't only performance, it was personality, too. Why, there are over 200 Top Fuelers in the world who aren't as well known as I am, and I'm not saying I'm better than them all, but it sure helps because I'm a gal. People love to see a gal beat the boys—that's what I call them, 'the boys.' Even when I was a kid I always had the brass to race the boys, although that's not why I really got started. I didn't begin all this 'beating the boys' stuff' until I saw how I could capitalize on it. Now I make a point of it. Oh, they throw tantrums. They beat their helmets on their cars, and some of 'em swear they'll drive their cars off a cliff if I beat them. Oh, for sure, they hated to race me. And it's a big advantage for me on the starting line. When

Gary Beck pulls alongside of me, he's not only thinking about his car but also that he's racing me, a woman, and no matter what he says it's always there in his mind and it upsets him. Oh, I just freak those boys out!"

Today, the advantages of being a woman drag racer far outweigh the disadvantages for Shirley. She is lighter than most of her competitors, which is a decided advantage, and although she admits she is not as knowledgeable about her car as some drivers with a mechanical background, she claims to have "a feel for my car" that they do not. "It's like an animal to me," she says. "I feel I have a tiger by the tail, it's something alive. Of course, the other drivers would laugh at me."

Shirley is also not averse to using what most men would call "her feminine wiles" to her advantage both as a driver and as a personality. She makes a point of using different engine parts from most of the famous engine builders, rather than using the parts exclusively of one builder. "I don't want to be known as an 'Ed Pink car,' she says, or a 'Keith Black car,' which I would if I used their parts exclusively. This way I stay independent. I have my own identity when I win. Of course the boys treat me like a queen, it's like having three or four suitors—Sid Waterman, Ed Pink, Keith Black, you know. Behind my back, though, they accuse me of being very tough, foul-mouthed, oh they call me some doosies. They claim I'm just image conscious, but they don't realize how much work goes into it, talking to all those reporters and everything. Most of them don't want to bother with reporters. Now Donald (Garlits) can be very short with people, you know. He's years ahead of the rest of us as far as racing goes, but he is kinda short with the press. And his car, oh, it's stone ugly. He calls it 'The Swamp Rat.' Some of the guys paint obscene women on their cars, and that's bitchin', everyone to his own thing, but I can't paint an obscene guy on my car. I just can't."

Shirley's flair for the press release was what prompted her to accept an invitation recently to appear in the Women's Superstars competition despite the fact that she admits "I'm no athlete." She finished dead last in every event, she says, including the quarter mile race, which she completed even though she did have to "stop and take a rest every so often. Oh, I competed against all those heavy hitters, Martina Navra . . . whatever her name is, and Althea Gibson, who is such a perfect lady. She would throw the basketball over her head without even facing the basket and it would go in while I, well, I couldn't even hit the backboard. Would you believe my best softball throw was 76 feet, and the winner threw it 176 feet? I mean, they were like union stewards."

In addition to her Superstars invitation ("I did it for my sport," she says.), Shirley's fame as Cha-Cha Muldowney has brought her other rewards, such as a yearly income in six figures and the kind of recognition she never stopped dreaming of obtaining. She has been a guest on such television programs as "What's My

Line?" and "To Tell the Truth," and she is still recognized for an English Leather cologne television commercial she once did in which she wore an asbestos fire suit while standing beside her lethal-looking Top Fuel dragster. Here she pulled off her spaceman's helmet, shook her head like a colt to unmat her hair and then, looking her sultry best, said in clipped tones, "All my men wear English Leather or else they wear nothing at all." (Always the woman of the 1950s, Shirley says, "It's not something I particularly enjoyed saying. However . . .")

There are other things Shirley Muldowney loves about being Cha-Cha. She loves the travel, the perpetual state of flux her life is in, of always being on the move whether it is moving along a desolate highway outside of Phoenix in her flat bed truck with her puppy beside her on the seat, or moving around greater Los Angeles, hustling for parts from Ed Pink and Keith Black or finally moving down a drag strip at a speed in excess of 250 mph. Her life as Cha-Cha is one of constant exhilaration, a state Shirley Rocque was determined to experience ever since she ran away to New York City at the age of thirteen.

"My sister is a housewife," she says. "She's never been anywhere, done anything. Most housewives my age, their lives are going downhill. My life is exciting. I love my life. I love hustling for parts and living out of a suitcase and being on television and stopping every once in awhile in New York City. I get up at six o'clock in the morning to see the garbage men. I go to a deli for breakfast and then just walk around the deserted streets looking at everything. New York City is a great place to go for someone who doesn't really have any place to go. It's a place for everyone, for morphodites, for anyone who wants to get their shit together. But what I love most about my life is the racing. I love to race. There is no feeling in the world like pulling to a starting line at dusk at some fairgrounds someplace. There are twenty cars behind you and you know this is your last chance to qualify. You can see the flames coming out of all eight exhaust pipes and it's the most beautiful sight in the world! And the noise, like an animal, oh, it just turns me on. It's hard to explain, really, how exciting it is. It's not only the competition, the beating someone, but it's this very light feeling you get, like dropping very fast in an elevator. You can flat tell a perfect pass, you can just feel it! Time is suspended. Everything slows down and five seconds becomes a very long time."

Broken Patterns

PART I

"I walked out on him. We weren't getting along anyway. When I told my parents they refused to talk to me. My students asked me why. I told them I was leaving to play volleyball. They couldn't understand. But *why*, they kept asking, *why* did I have to leave my husband, my home, my job, *everything*, just for a game? I couldn't explain it. I told them I didn't know why but that I was leaving anyway, to become a volleyball bum."

Sunlight through an open window illuminates faint particles of dust suspended in smoky golden shafts that fan out and down over the polished hardwood floor. The floor is bare except for the cardboard patterns of a dress scattered across the floor in disarray. At one end of the sparsely furnished room is a sewing machine. Seated behind it is a woman in her late twenties sewing a piece of cloth by hand. She is looking down at the cloth in her lap, her head tilted in such a way that her features are foreshortened and shadowed. Only her hair is caught by the smoky shafts of light. Spun-gold curls explode with sunlight, blaze like a burning bush whose golden fires diffuse her body in a hazy nimbus.

"I drove to Houston. I'd heard about Mary Jo through the grapevine. Everyone in volleyball knew about her. All the girls on her team lived in a big old house in Houston. Mary Jo did the cooking. I remember one day she left some pots boiling on the stove. One of the girls turned them off. Mary Jo was furious. *She* was the cook, she said, and locked herself in her room. A few weeks later I walked into the kitchen and there were three girls staring at a pot of stew. The stew was bubbling and boiling over the sides of the pot down the side of the stove and onto the floor. Mary Jo had gone out and had forgotten to turn it off. None of the girls would touch it. "Not me," said one of the girls. "You think I'm crazy!" They just stared at it until she came back. We were terrified of her. She was so hard on us. But we were all very emotionally involved with her, too. We looked to her for direction, both as players and as women. She was going to lead us to an Olympic gold medal. It was our dream. Then they took the program away from her. Just like *that!* We had nothing left. *Nothing!* She was almost *suicidal!*"

The woman does not lift up her head as she talks. She continues to stare down at the cloth in her lap as if

talking to it, and as she does she repeatedly stabs it with
the needle—quick, darting, vicious stabs. The man she
is talking to is at the opposite end of the room. They are
separated by the shafts of sunlight. He is in the shadows,
distinguishable merely as a dark form seated on a
couch. He is sitting forward on the edge of his seat, his
back rigid, his elbows propped on his knees, his hands
folded at his chin. He is perfectly still, has not spoken
a word or moved a muscle in so long that his body feels
leaden. And yet he is lightheaded, spinning, his heart
pounding so wildly in his chest that he is afraid she will
hear the beating and sense how excited he has become
by her monologue. He is afraid, too, that she will crack
soon. Her voice has grown shrill without her having
realized it. Her words are spilling out faster and faster,
in rhythm almost with her stabbing needle, her arm
attacking the cloth with such swiftness and force, like
a cobra, that he sees only a pink blur before it strikes.
It has occurred to him, a stranger, that he is no longer
just her sympathetic listener but has become, in her
mind's eye, the cause and the object of her frustration.
She is talking breathlessly fast now, without inflection,
simply spewing out word after word as if, like him, she
is afraid that if she pauses the barest split second she
will collapse into hysterical sobbings, will never finish
her lament, will lose, irrevocably, this opportunity to
get it all out into the open, just as it has been these past
years, perfectly shaped and formed inside her. She is
also fearful that the slightest hesitation will allow him

to break the spell, to change the subject, to ask some inconsequential question that will expose his obvious insensitivity to this moment, that will, in fact, reaffirm her belief in that insensitivity. She would take great satisfaction in such an exposure. At any other moment in her life she might deliberately pause, deliberately elicit from him an example of his lack. But not now. Not at this moment. She suppresses her desire for revenge and opts instead for the satisfaction of revealing her lament, the truth.

"We were *all* suicidal so emotionally attached to her . . . but she can't see it . . . she's such a dreamer. When they took away her program, everything, she was so hurt, she just quit volleyball . . . she had gone through hell to play volleyball . . . her parents had deserted her. Now she's turned professional . . . she's going to play with a new pro team here in El Paso . . . she'll be one of two women on a men's team . . . she won't be able to adjust to men . . . they're *so* insensitive. They told me if I hung around El Paso at my own expense they might put me on the taxi squad. I'd sacrifice everything for the Olympics, sacrifice myself on the court for the good of the team and for Mary Jo, but I could never do that for money on a team with men. They'll try to dominate her and she won't let them . . . she'll never adjust . . . she's light-years ahead of them in her thinking. When it comes to volleyball plays and systems, she's a genius . . . but in other ways she's a dreamer. She was the best of coaches and the worst of coaches . . . she had these beautiful systems all worked out in her head, but we could never perform them on the court and she could never understand why."

On page 25 of the March 1975 issue of *womenSports* magazine there is a photograph of Mary Jo Peppler, a thirty-one-year-old volleyball player. She is dressed in sweat pants and a halter jersey that exposes a bare shoulder and a muscular arm. She is carrying a leather satchel-like pocketbook tossed carelessly over one shoulder. It is a shadowy, unposed-for shot that has caught her standing sideways, staring out over her left shoulder. The expression on that shadowed face is at once so severe and threatening that it seems its possessor were instinctively wary, as if at that very moment she were trying to read each and every viewer of that picture—potential antagonists—even as they were reading her. She has short, dark, pixie-cut hair that falls over her forehead but stops just above thick, linear eyebrows, which overline her narrowed eyes. She has the eyes of a comic strip villain, straight on top and curved below, like half-moons. She has a broad, upturned nose and a large, shapely mouth, the lips parted slightly to expose two prominent front teeth. Her lips curl back from those teeth in such a way as to hint at bared fangs. Her entire facial expression, in fact, appears to be one emanating from within rather than merely imposed on her by the natural shape and arrangement of her features. But despite their threatening cast, they reveal an exceptionally attractive woman in that bold, high-cheekboned, Slavic way so typical of Eastern Europeans.

The article accompanying that photograph of Mary Jo Peppler describes a woman who is an extremely talented athlete and coach, and who is every bit as threatening as her demeanor suggests. An amateur volleyball player for the past twelve years, she has, among other accomplishments, been voted the best woman player in the world at the 1970 World Games in Bulgaria despite the fact that her U.S. team finished eleventh. According to Val Keller, coach of the Americans, "She *is* the best woman volleyball player in the world, bar none."

As a coach herself she formed two of the most powerful women's teams in the country, the Los Angeles Renegades and the E Pluribus Unum team of Houston. Her Houston-based team won back-to-back U.S. championships in 1972 and '73, to wrest that title from its perennial Southern California possessors for the first time in twenty-two years.

Despite such playing and coaching successes, Mary Jo Peppler's volleyball career has been filled with controversy. She has sustained a running feud with the hierarchy of the U.S. Volley Ball Association in what she claims is her quest to improve the caliber of American teams, eventually to bring an Olympic gold medal to the United States, and most importantly to wrest control of women's volleyball from the nonplaying executives of the USVBA and deposit that control where she feels it rightly belongs, with the players and coaches. Because of her incessant demands on and her aloof attitude toward the USVBA hierarchy, she has been accused of being a prima donna who either quits when she does not get her way or who "slacks off" during competition as a show of petulance. Such unpredictable behavior earned her this comment from Al Monaco, executive director of the USVBA: "She's a gifted athlete who can't be handled."

Mary Jo Peppler finally proved herself so threatening a menace to the USVBA that she was stripped of her position as the assistant coach of the team that was to represent the U.S. in the 1976 Olympic Games and told that the USVBA was no longer interested in her services either as a player or a coach for the upcoming Games. The new U.S. coach, Charles Erbe, Jr., said he preferred to build his team around younger, more malleable women. "I've worked with older girls before," he said. "They did not have attitudes I wanted to train, and I told them to get lost."

Forced to abandon her dream of bringing an Olympic gold medal to the United States, Mary Jo Peppler retired temporarily from volleyball until formation of the professional International Volleyball Association. The new league, which began operating in June 1975 in such cities as Santa Barbara, San Diego, Los Angeles, and El Paso-Juarez is funded by film producer David Wolper and Motown record magnate Berry Gordy. It will field co-ed teams consisting of two women and four men. Mary Jo Peppler was one of the most sought-after women for this new league, and she signed a contract with the El Paso-Juarez Sols, which officially ended her amateur career and any hopes she had of ever playing on an Olympic gold medal team.

At the time she signed that contract she was still the best woman volleyball player in the world and still, after twelve years, relatively unknown as an athlete in her native country. Two months later she won the first Women's Superstar Competition in Rotunda, Florida, defeating such famous women athletes as Billy Jean King, Micki King, Kathy Rigby and Diane Hollum, along with less well-known but equally talented women such as Joan Joyce, Karen Logan and Wyomia Tyus. Many of the most knowledgeable people in sport who witnessed her performances in the various Superstar events claim that she is quite possibly the greatest all-around woman athlete in this country today, and maybe in the world. At the age of thirty-one, then, after a lifetime devoted to sport and its excellence for which she received anonymity, Mary Jo Peppler was finally thrust before the public's eye for what may have been only a fleeting moment.

The Brazos Hotel in downtown El Paso is a square four-story stucco building painted the color of mustard. It is both dwarfed and shadowed by the city's glass-and-chrome skyscrapers and, at the same time, set apart from them by the spacious parking lots that surround it on all sides. The Brazos is a lost island deserted by time. It belongs to another El Paso—a flat, dusty, bleached, unshadowed desert town shimmering and floating under a blazing-white sun, a town of hot dry winds and skipping sagebrush and adobe huts with shuttered windows like black holes, a town of Mexican women and gunfights and then quick flights on horseback through the desert beneath the moving shadows of the Rocky Mountains and, finally, with luck, safety in Juarez. The Brazos belongs to the El Paso of outlaws.

Today's El Paso is a towering city of reflecting glass that blocks out the sun and creates pockets of cool shade on the sidewalks. It is a modern, international city situated in the extreme southwestern corner of the state. The population is almost equal parts of native Texans, many of whom can trace their ancestry back to the pioneers, and Mexican-Americans, who can trace their ancestry farther back to the Incas. In any group of pedestrians downtown, one is struck by that look of the Incas—polished black hair, slitlike eyes resting on Inca cheekbones, jawlines that balloon out like the bottom half of a pear, and bodies that tend to be short, round and without the definition of a waist. Because the two races have mingled amicably enough over the years, most El Pasoans look to the south of Juarez, Mexico, and to the west of New Mexico for their business and pleasurable pursuits, rather than to the east and the rest of Texas, which they view as a foreign land having not the slightest meaning in their lives. El Pasoans consider themselves Southwesterners who are only geographically attached to a southern state. In their eyes, the Texas of Houston and Dallas-Ft. Worth belongs to the Deep South of rednecks and bigots, of heavy millionaires in ivory-colored Continentals whose hoods are festooned with longhorns. In El Paso the millionaires are younger men, lean and athletic, in their forties. They wear western shirts and jeans to work, and instead of cowboy boots they wear Puma track shoes. Driving new Volkswagen Sciroccos, they see themselves as outlaws from the rest of their state. And, in truth, El Paso is still an outlaw town, a refuge for occasional dissident athletes. Ben Jipcho, the miler, abandoned his native Kenya in order to compete for El Paso on the pro track tour; and Mary Jo Peppler, the volleyball star, fled a dream lost in the tropical foliage of Houston for the uncertainty of a new lifestyle in the limitless desert of El Paso.

Across the street from the Brazos Hotel on a bright spring afternoon, Mary Jo Peppler, wearing a gray t-shirt, jeans and sneakers, steps off the curb, makes a sideways tossing gesture with her head like a colt does, and crosses the street. Behind her, waiting for the traffic light to change, a group of Mexican pedestrians stares after the towering white woman. She is almost 6'1" tall, although she is so well proportioned at 155 pounds that from a distance one is not conscious of her height. She crosses the street with long strides, her upper body held regally stiff, arched backward almost, while her lower body seems to swivel left and right as if, with each step, she were crushing out cigarette butts with the balls of her feet. She steps up onto the curb, navigates the steps of the Brazos two at a time and enters the building.

Like all the doors in the Brazos, the door to her apartment on the second floor is marked by a lion's head door knocker. Inside, the apartment is bright and spacious, with whitewashed walls and tall windows that fill the living room with sunlight. There is a sofa in the center of the room. Drooping over one arm of the sofa is a chromed tentacle-limbed lamp. By the windows sits a fan-shaped, high-backed wicker chair such as one expects to see in every Tennessee Williams play. Beside the chair is a towering potted plant with oily and rubbery-looking leaves. There is an Oriental tapestry on one wall, a portable television set on a movable stand, a small fireplace, a pile of cellophane-wrapped artificial logs and, alongside the fireplace, a few more potted plants, smaller than the others and with leaves that are dying. Everything in that apartment, including the appliances in the kitchen, looks newly purchased, not yet broken in, the furniture of someone used to renting furnished rooms and for whom these new purchases are the first conscious attempts at permanence. And yet even after three months, the apartment is so bright and spare, without the untidy minutiae of daily living, that one suspects this attempt is still unnatural to its inhabitant, is still only a halting half-step forward while the back leg is tensed for flight. In the kitchen the new dishwasher is not hooked up yet; in the bedroom the clothes' closet is merely a large upright suitcase that can, at a moment's notice, be folded up, snapped shut and carted off; in the small room off the living room there is the clutter of not-yet-sorted-out odds and ends —a new chrome pulley exercise machine, powder blue weights, cartons of paperback books (astrology, short stories, volleyball techniques), an ironing board and, in the corner of the room, a gray filing cabinet.

Everything in that filing cabinet—newspaper clippings, magazine articles, outlines, notes, etc.—pertains to one of four topics: volleyball, women, women in sport, or sport in general. It also contains an outline for a prospective book dealing with these four topics that its author has been working on for the better part of ten years. That outline, written in the staccato sports jargon of the academician ("Atmosphere" vs. Direct Verbalization), begins with an attempt by its author to identify and define certain characteristics indigenous only to American athletes (i.e., prone to "hero worship") and then to use those characteristics to create a typically American style of volleyball play. Among the many claims its author makes is the following: American athletes are generally superior to athletes of other nationalities, but for various reasons (lack of proper training or dedication, for example) this superiority does not always surface in international competition.

The second and most important part of that outline, titled "Communication and Handling the Woman Athlete Within the Team Framework," is an attempt to identify and define certain psychological differences between males and females and then either to eliminate or channel those differences as they exist in women in order to help them become superior athletes. Among its many claims are the following: women are taught to talk about their problems rather than deal with them overtly (i.e., boys-fight, girls-indirect); women can solve their problems only when they are brought into the open by a crisis; women are taught to be nonaggressive, idealistic and servile; women appear to be easily dominated, easily influenced by authority figures, easily trained to please, and generally more concerned with external approval (from others) than internal approval (from themselves). It also claims that male coaches have difficulty dealing with women athletes because men are not as sensitive as women; men have such low expectations of women that they are too easily impressed by meager achievements; men are basically egoists who thrive on domination as opposed to women who are altruists trained to be submissive; and finally, men feel threatened by a show of strength in women be it physical or internal.

The author feels that most of the female traits defined in this section are learned traits, and so can be unlearned or redirected in such a way as to improve a female athlete's performance. Hidden beneath the surface of this stated goal is one infinitely more subtle and sweeping. It is an attempt by the author to reshape women, into a self-image more pleasing than any they have ever endured.

Seated Indian-style on the floor in front of her fireplace, Mary Jo Peppler fingers the dried crumbling leaves of her plants and says, "Where am I from? Nowhere, really. My father was a traveling pharmaceutical-supplies salesman so we never lived more than three years in any one place. I was born in Illinois but lived in Pennsylvania, Rhode Island, Texas and California before I was ten years old. I spent most of my teenage years in the San Fernando Valley and Long Beach in Southern California. Anywhere I went, though, I was inclined to get into sports. It's always been a part of my life since I can remember. I played all the sports with the boys—I was the quarterback on our neighborhood football team—until about the sixth grade, when my parents told me I shouldn't be out there playing football with the boys, taking off my t-shirt and all, you know. It was a tough day for me when they told me that. Sports in school weren't very competitive for girls, just what they called 'play days.' We'd play all different sports without even keeping score. It was felt that competition was bad for girls. They wouldn't allow any men to get involved in our sports as coaches or officials because then they'd bring with them the idea of competition. It was something women were afraid of. Sports for girls, then, were just a way to get exercise.

"By the time I got to high school it was obvious I had

talent compared to the other people in school. But no-
body directed me. If I had had any kind of encouragement at all I would have been smart to go into a more
recognizable sport, like tennis, rather than volleyball. I
did go out for a girls' softball team once, but I didn't like
the type of girls they had. They were too tough. Volleyball was more a group sport with us. All the guys and
girls would pile into an old Volvo and go to the park and
play volleyball together. It was a social thing. The guys
and girls played on the same team. We never played
much at the beach, though. That kind of volleyball has
a different connotation from the kind we played. That's
a whole lifestyle—sun-and-surf and all—that we were
never into. By my junior year I was good enough to play
for the Long Beach Shamrocks, the women's National
Champions. I played all of 1962 with them, but when
they went to the Nationals they left me home and took
older players. I felt I was as good as any girls they took,
so I quit and joined the second best team around, the
L.A. Spartans. Two years later I helped form the Los
Angeles Renegades, and we won the AAU National
Championship.

"It was about this time, I was seventeen I guess, that
I met Baylor Farkis, a Hungarian track coach. He said
he thought I could be a great decathlon athlete, and so
he began grooming me in shot-putting, javelin throwing, hurdling—all the decathlon events. That year I
finished seventh in the nation in the javelin and fourth
in the shot. I competed only because the United States

wasn't qualified for the Olympics in volleyball. But when Brazil dropped out of the '64 volleyball trials and the U.S. was picked to replace them, I dropped the decathlon. I think I would have made a good decathlon person, too, if I'd kept at it. But I would have had to do things I didn't want to do. Shot-putters are really heavy, you know, and I didn't want to bulk up. There's no way you can bulk up without becoming half-man, half-woman. I would have had to give up my femininity for sport. Do you remember Tamara Press, the Russian gold medalist? She, or he, or whatever, was just, well, you know, when they started doing sex tests she disappeared. Looking at her, I don't think she could have passed them. Besides, who wants to be a shot-putter? You just push the thing out there. It's not too exciting. Now, volleyball is stimulating, it's in a child's state of development in this country. There are things I can do with it—new systems and possibilities—that are exciting.

"It was about this time that I left home. I was seventeen or eighteen I think. My parents were moving to San Francisco and I wouldn't go. I told them there was no way I'd make the Olympic team if I moved to San Francisco. There was a big argument and all, and we didn't talk for five or six years. They thought I was sincere in my effort, but they just didn't think I'd make it. Maybe, too, they didn't think my ambitions were proper for a girl. I had never got any encouragement or discouragement from either parent, although my father was a well-known golfer. He pushed my brother into sports, and I think my brother always resented it. When my parents left I moved in with the family of a female javelin thrower. I took jobs like selling encyclopedias door-to-door. I sold to low-income houses and I was supposed to force-sell them. I couldn't do it. I could sell fine to an educated area where people needed them, but how could I sell an expensive set of encyclopedias to houses with trash on the lawn and sixteen kids' wagons on the sidewalk? I sold candy for a while after that, and then I worked in a department store. I never regretted leaving home. I always felt like I could make my own decisions for myself. I've always felt I was mature, independent and smart enough to run myself.

"When I graduated from high school I went to Los Angeles State as a psychology major. What do I feel about my childhood? I had a whole theory about it once, but I don't remember what it is now. I was fairly free, I guess. My parents gave me some values that were sound to operate from. There are traits all my brothers and sisters have. We're independent and confident. We were all expected to finish college and we did, although it took me nine years. I was playing volleyball for nothing and supporting myself, so whenever I got into a crunch and had to give up something, it was always school, of course. But it never occurred to me not to finish.

"I made the '64 volleyball team that went to the

Olympics, but it was a disaster. We'd been a last-second replacement for Brazil and we had had only three weeks practice. Our coach was an old-timer who had been given the job just because it was his turn. All he would ever say to us was, "Bend your knees, honey!" Volleyball is an American sport, it originated here, but it's been dominated by foreign teams who take it more seriously. They've helped change the rules to their advantage, to make the best use of their particular styles of play, especially the Japanese. Well, we finished fifth of six teams there, but I wasn't particularly impressed. I wasn't impressed with any of the athletes at the Olympics. They didn't seem very athletic. The Japanese, for example, could play volleyball, jump and dive and all, but they couldn't even run. I don't think there was an athlete there who had anything more than me, except better training. I think, in general, Americans are better natural athletes than any other nationality in the world. We just aren't developed enough.

"Four years later I quit the '68 Olympic team for the same reason. The coach had no game plans or strategy, and I saw no reason to be humiliated in international competition while the whole world was watching. After that I didn't play volleyball for a while and wasn't doing much of anything until a friend of mine, Marilyn McReavy, talked me into going to college with her at Sul Ross State University in Alpine, Texas. It was kind of an escape from volleyball. I took courses in photography, lapidary, upholstery, Egyptian philosophy, things

I liked. Eventually I majored in both phys ed and sociology and minored in industrial arts. I supported myself as a secretary and a saleswoman in a department store, and I had no intention of returning to volleyball. However, word got around that Olympic volleyball players, Marilyn and I, were at Sul Ross, so they asked us to stage an exhibition against anyone who'd challenge us. The people had never really seen top-notch volleyball. We got a whole gym full of fans to watch us play these big ole football players and cowboys. The cowboys played with their hats on. We killed them. We bounced balls off their heads and everything. The fans loved it.

"One month later we had organized a team of Sul Ross girls to go to the national tournament. The girls were so totally inexperienced that we only had time to teach them elemental moves. We finished eighth that year. The following year we won the National Collegiate championship. By 1972 we had formed the E Pluribus Unum team in Houston, and for the first time in twenty-two years a California team was defeated for the national title. At that time the USVBA had just made a rule that the best team in the nation would represent the U.S. at the Olympics rather than an all-star team of the best players in the nation. I'd been fighting for this unity concept rather than all-star concept for years. After we had won the title from California, the favorite, to be the U.S. representatives, we were supposed to go on a volleyball tour to Peru in preparation for the Olympics. The USVBA canceled the tour. I could see what was developing—a power play—and so I told the USVBA unless we had our way and certain changes were made in the program, we wouldn't compete in the Olympics. We didn't, and the U.S. failed to qualify a volleyball team in '72. "EPU—E Pluribus Unum—won the nationals again in '73, and the Olympic program was transferred to us in Houston. However, in another power play, the USVBA forced Marilyn and me, the coaches, to take on a new head coach, a man. We became his assistants. At the time we had guided the EPU team to a 72–0 record in two years. The USVBA put pressure on this new coach to take control of the girls from us. In June of '73 we went on what was just supposed to be a training tour to Japan, but everything fell apart. We finished with a 1–24 record against the Japanese teams. Marilyn and I lost control of the girls. Their personal and playing standards deteriorated, and the new coach couldn't control them. He turned into a crazy man. One night he sat under a tree wearing dark glasses until the following morning. He wore dark glasses everywhere. He wouldn't talk to us. And to make matters worse, he had an emotional thing going with one of the girls. When we finally returned from Japan the USVBA fired him, gave our team to a new coach, Charles Zerbe, and he told the older girls like Marilyn and myself to get lost. It was then that I quit amateur volleyball for good. A few months later I signed a contract with the El Paso-Juarez Sols.

"The most bitter disappointment in my life was sign-
ing that professional contract. I had devoted my life to
the dream of winning a gold medal for the United
States in volleyball. I'd left my family because of that.
And over all those years I had never really been given
a chance. Not even a chance! It was always lousy coaching and stuff, always trying to escape the inevitable. I
was the only player the USVBA wanted for a long time.
But I refused to go. I was preserving my ego from loss.
If I did my best and we lost, O.K. But I never had the
feeling I could do my best in those situations. I never
really felt I had a fair chance to compete. And yet,
when I had to face the decision to turn pro, I could
hardly force myself to do it. There were so many people
depending on me in an amateur sense as coach and as
a leader. I'd been brainwashing the girls into believing
an Olympic gold medal was really something worth
aiming for. We trained six hours a day in an empty gym
and we'd never even got a chance. Even after we lost
it, I wouldn't give in at first. On the night we found out,
all the girls went out for dinner at a pizza restaurant.
I got there late. The girls were drinking. They would
never have had a drink in front of me before, not even
beer. It really upset me. I realized that they had been
following me only for the medal and not because volleyball was a way of life. That's really what I'd been
trying to instill in them. It wasn't just the medal, or
volleyball, or even sport. It *was* a whole way of life. I
deliberately ordered just a glass of milk in front of

them. They put down their drinks and before long everyone had ordered either soda or milk. I had made a commitment to those girls, not by anything I said but by my actions and my lifestyle. That was why it was such a hard thing to tell them I was becoming a professional.

"I'm glad I did it now. There are so many things wrong with amateur athletics in this country. It's absurd to be an amateur. There are so few rewards. Even a gold medal, what the hell does it mean? It has no lasting value. Sometimes I'm not sure if there's anything good about being idealistically dedicated to amateur sports. It's self-defeating to be an amateur athlete today, and that's basically what most women athletes are—amateurs."

PART II

The business office of El Paso Pro Sports, Incorporated, a concern that handles the affairs of the El Paso-Juarez Sols of the newly-formed professional International Volleyball Association and the El Paso entry on the pro track tour, is located on the nineteenth floor of the First Federal Bank Building of El Paso, a glass-and-chrome skyscraper in the heart of the city. The office consists of a network of many small rooms, all of whose doors seem perpetually ajar so that its occupants can shout to each other without resorting to the intercom system. It is one of those loosely run offices where the receptionist never seems to be at her desk, so anyone—lawyers, athletes, public relations men, journalists, strangers— can just wander down the corridors, at will. Still, the effect is not one of disorganization but of casualness. Most of the action and noise on any given day emanates from the small, disheveled office of the president of El Paso Pro Sports, James K. Brennand, a forty-year-old lawyer and millionaire. Strewn among his important papers are an old copy of *Playboy* magazine, a hard-cover edition of Irving Wallace's *The Fan Club*, and a newly opened bottle of Haitian rum. Dominating one entire wall of the office is a blackboard (green, actually) listing the names of all the foreign volleyball players eligible for the upcoming IVA draft. To any but the most avid fans, the names on that board are unfamiliar—Soo Koo Lee, Kim Kon Bong, Vogel Sang, Meliton Jiminez, Peter and Isabella Petrov.

One recent spring day, Brennand was seated at his desk alternately sipping from a mug of coffee and talking on the telephone to an editor of the *National Star* newspaper. He is a trim, handsome, well-tanned man whose sandy hair is styled in a short, shaggy cut. He resembles, not so much in features but in the sensual and lethargic way he moves and talks, Dean Martin. He has none of Martin's oiliness, however, nor his look of dissipation, and in fact appears to be a remarkably vigorous man. He had been a successful lawyer in El Paso at a very early age, had left his practice to live in England for a few years, then had returned to El Paso where he became involved with El Paso Pro Sports, Inc. He has become physically immersed in most of the sports with which he deals. He is one of those men who is always trying to scare up a handball game at noon, a tennis match after work, a volleyball game after dinner. He competes enthusiastically, although in that mechanically correct rather than instinctive way of men who have come to such games late in life. He seems always open to learn, whether about volleyball or tennis or the people with whom he is dealing. That openness, however, seems not so much a natural, unbounded exuberance as it is a conscious and meticulous effort. He is a single-focus sort of man too easily distracted. He once spent an hour composing a note informing a friend as to his whereabouts later in the day. Now he is dressed in jeans, a western shirt and, around his neck, a tight strand of love beads. Behind him is a plate-glass window affording a breathtaking view of El Paso and the limitless sands that surround it. Far off in the distance but looming massive and jagged, are the Rocky Mountains. The shadows of those mountains still seem to be alive, moving across the desert exactly as they had once moved when outlaws fled to the safety of Juarez.

Brennand says into the telephone, "Now, jes' what's that supposta mean?" His voice, though soft and lazy, is still exasperated by something he has just heard and by the fact that he is having difficulty sustaining his concentration amid the many boisterous conversations around him. Talking at once in his office are: Wayne

Vandenberg, a florid-faced, euphoric man who was once a Utah track coach and who helped prepare Mary Jo Peppler for the Superstars competition; J. J. Jackson, a jive-talking black sprinter dressed entirely in kelly green (suit, vest, tie and patent-leather clogs); Carrie Ellison, a lean, long-limbed miler with the pale features of Kier Dullea; Horace Smitty-Duke, a muscular, western-looking man with a wavy pompadour, who was once an All-American volleyball player from Dallas and is now the playing head coach of the Sols; and a writer who has abandoned any hope of following all these conversations and so has just flicked on his tape recorder, folded his arms across his chest and sat back in his chair.

"You gotta have the threads," says Jackson to Ellison. "It's the only way to go, man."

Vandenberg is saying to the writer, "We figured if the weakest link in this new co-ed volleyball concept is gonna be the women than we'd better go out and find the strongest woman volleyball player in the world. And she's strong, you know what I mean, S-T-R-O-N-G. We'd heard she was tough to handle, but that's because she's a perfectionist. She dedicated her life to playing volleyball. If she was a rebel it was because she wanted to be the best. She's a doer, not a committee person. She always had to fight to assume leadership in the USVBA but now, as a pro, she has the opportunity to be a spokesman for the IVA. That's why she turned pro. She decided she was finished as an amateur."

"He's unreal!" says Ellison to Jackson. He is talking

about fellow miler Ben Jipcho. "The way he trains! He asked me if I wanted to run with him one day. I said, 'Sure.' So he takes me out to the mountains and, whoosh, he takes off at full speed. He runs full speed up the mountain until he drops. Then the next day he does the same thing, only this time he runs a little further before he drops. That's how he increases his endurance. And here I am running with a nice steady stride, you know, pacing myself. I didn't believe it until I saw it."

"In L.A. it's a beach-bum kinda life," says Smitty-Duke. "You know, surfing and hot dogging it on the beach. In Texas it's a sport."

Brennand hangs up the receiver and says to no one in particular, "Now whadn't that sumthin'? What the hell kinda paper is the *National Star* anyway? I never heard of it. This guys says he wants a picture of Mary Jo. 'Sexy,' he says, 'but not too extreme.' What's that supposta mean? No bra, topless? Jeezes, we're trying to project a proper image here. Understated but elegant."

"I don't think we'll have any problems communicating," says Smitty-Duke to the writer. He is referring to Mary Jo Peppler. "She'll be my assistant coach. There's a lot we can learn from one another. Still, I'm aware of her past reputation."

"I don't think there's anything to worry about," interjects Brennand. "Mary Jo's changing her opinions. She realizes negativism is harmful. Still, she's her own person. You don't quote Mary Jo for her to the press. I'll bet I could give quotes for almost any male athlete and they'd be pretty accurate, but not for her. She's an original thinker. She's had all those years of anonymity to develop her ideas. There's nothing more enjoyable than a one-to-one two-hour lunch with her. It's an incredible experience. You get down to that beautiful, intelligent mind of hers."

"And she's so strong," says Vandenberg. "You see a woman do something strong and you say, 'Just like a man.' But nothing Mary Jo does in sport is 'just like a man.' She's strong but still in a feminine way."

"Jes' 'cause she can beat you in arm wrestling dodn't mean she's a masculine person," says Brennand. "Her strength has feminine aspects to it, if you know what I mean. She's got beautiful legs. The No-nonsense pantyhose people want her for a commercial. After her victory in the Superstars thing she's gotten all kinds of offers. *The Ladies' Home Journal* wants her to do a column and to use her picture on the cover. She's got offers to appear on the "AM America Show" on ABC-TV and on the Johnny Carson show with McLean Stevenson. I told her winning the Superstars is a six-figure venture. It can become a second career. She's supposta go to New York City on Tuesday, but I don't know. I'm kinda worried about her goin'. It's cold up there. She don't even own a winter coat. She's never been outta the South before. She could get mugged, raped, Lord knows what! She dodn't even know how to pay for a taxi. Evertime we go someplace she pulls a ten-dollar bill outta her pocketbook like she's gonna pay. 'Who the hell you kiddin'?' I always tell her. 'You been carryin' that same crumpled ole ten-dollar bill around with you for years, Mary Jo. That's the way you athletes are.' "

At the Brazos Hotel, Mary Jo Peppler and a friend, Carol Dewey, a tall, pale woman with fluffy blonde curls, have just finished stacking the last of a shipment of wooden planks in the living room of her second-floor apartment. Carol gets down on her knees and begins to count the planks. Standing over her, Mary Jo says, "Carol's my carpenter person. She's going to build a desk for me."

Looking up, smiling, Carol says, "I love to work with my hands. I'd be happy if I could do this for the rest of my life. I used to be a schoolteacher, but I left it to become a volleyball bum."

A blank look descends on Mary Jo's face. After a momentary pause she says in a voice devoid of inflection, "What does that mean? 'Volleyball Bum.' "

"It's just a term, Mary Jo. You know what I mean."

"No, I don't. If it means giving up your life for no rewards, if it means never having any money and always being on the move, if it means living a nomadic life—then maybe in that sense it is like being a bum." Carol returns to the wood and resumes her counting. No one talks for a while.

Much later, alone, Mary Jo says, "It *has* been a hassle all these years, scrubbing around to support myself, half the time living in a poverty state just to play volleyball.

It's hard on your psychological well-being. There were always so many things I wanted to do in sport. Now, hopefully, I'll be able to put some of those ideas into action. That's why if there was anything personally satisfying about winning the Superstars thing it was that it made me somewhat financially independent. I didn't much enjoy the actual competition, though. It wasn't any true test of an athlete—things like basketball shooting and rowing. I enjoyed meeting all those famous athletes. But as for the competition itself, I've gotten more satisfaction out of practicing volleyball in an empty gym. It's funny, though, when I think about it. Why me? I mean, all those other women had more notoriety than me. I was unknown, and yet at the trials in Houston I felt I was going to win. I *knew* I was. I took charge and did it. I won four events. I had power over it. That's the way my life's always been. Nothing ever just dropped on me. Still, when I got to Rotunda for the finals I didn't completely win by my control. Micki King and Karen Logan screwed up in events they were supposed to do well in, and then it all just came to me.

"Lately I've been thinking about that. I've been looking at all those different women and trying to see what they could do with their victory. It wouldn't mean much to Billy Jean. She's a great leader and all, she's made things happen for women in sport, but she's hung up on her own situation. Her attitudes are very masculine—success and money. She was in the public eye at a very young age, at an age when she should have been constantly forming new ideas instead of projecting an image. I was fortunate to be protected from being a public image for all these years. I wasn't forced to become something before I was ready. When people have an image of you sometimes you unconsciously try to fulfill that image rather than thinking your way through to new attitudes. Karen Logan, too, looked like she was in the best position to beat me. But what could she do with it? She said sports had given her confidence. She talked only in personal terms. This was it for her. She could become famous, rich. She had to win, she said, because her basketball career was dying. It was so sad. She had no organization, no thinking, nothing. Then I looked at Micki King. She was one of the most intellectual of all the women there. But her thinking is undeveloped in comparison to mine. She's still trying to reorganize amateur women's sports from the inside. That's immature. You have to break new ground outside of organized sport. What it all came down to, then, was me. It was a historic moment in women's sports and there were forces working for me. There are so many things I can do with this victory that the other's can't."

A few days later, Mary Jo Peppler receives a telephone call from a writer.

"We've talked a lot, "the writer says to her," and now I'd like to see how you move."

"You could take me dancing," she replies.

"Oh! Yeh," and he laughs weakly. He has been in El

Paso for three days now, has spent a good many hours with her, and still she confuses him. She confused him from the first moment he saw her at the airport. She was waiting for him by the baggage counter, a pretty woman in a sleeveless jersey and white slacks. She was extremely tall, well-tanned, grew even taller as he approached, was as tall as he! Big-boned. With long arms, muscled but without a man's definition. And yet, curiously, she did not look particularly athletic. A euphemism. He meant masculine, which was what he had expected. All the articles he had read about her dwelled on her size, her strength (stronger than most men, they claimed) and the severity of her nature. The tone of her quoted remarks alternated between flippancy ("Bring on Bob Seagren!") and brazen hostility ("I know a dozen girls who are better athletes than anyone here (Rotunda)"). And those photographs— almost frightening. In action, they showed a grim, straining, heavy-thighed woman; in repose, as in *womenSports,* they showed a woman distrustful and threatening, whose demeanor seemed deliberately calculated to wilt the most chauvinistic male. "Hard" was the word he would have used to describe her. And yet, the woman who greeted him at the airport was pretty with an open smile. She took one of his bags, the smaller one (he wondered why—deliberately, so as not to embarrass him?) and led him to her car. He said, "I'd like to stay someplace in close proximity to your apartment." He sounded so oppressively stuffed. "You can stay with me," she said. "Is that close enough?" She tossed his bag into the trunk of the car. He recalled his editor saying, "I don't know whether we want to mess with her. We heard her scene was trashy." And then, instinctively, he recalled the phrase "volleyball bum," with its lascivious and self-indulgent connotations. Was she defining future possibilities for them, he wondered, or was she merely being lighthearted? Only later did a third possibility occur to him. She might have been trying to put him at ease after his so obviously strained remark (". . . close proximity . . ."). But her voice had been curt, the words clipped off one by one without the inflection of lasciviousness or humor or even warmth, that he could read nothing into it beyond the mere words themselves. That's what confused him and would continue to confuse him for the next three days.

In conversation she spoke intimately about herself without suggesting intimacy. She spoke of her parents' desertion without showing any sense of the pain that desertion must have inflicted upon her. She spoke of all her experiences—pleasant and unpleasant—in the same tone so that *he* had to supply the subjective response—pain or pleasure. She told him about the time when she was eighteen but still naïve, when an old businessman had enticed her into his office, locked the door and begun to chase her around his desk. She eluded him easily. He grew exhausted, wheezing, his face bloated and purple. He offered her money, paused to catch a breath. She pointed an accusing finger at him and said, "You behave yourself! You have a bad heart. You'll get an attack." She did not leave until he had caught his breath. But even as she told this story, a simple act of kindness, she showed not the faintest compassion. It was just a story she was relating, leaving him to supply any nuances he might infer from it. Again, she mentioned a professional basketball star she'd once met, who suggested to her what she called "disgusting perversions," and yet even as she spoke that phrase neither her face nor her tone showed the faintest hint of disgust, which seemed for her merely a mental concept rather than an emotional one. Because she dealt on intellectual rather than emotional levels, it was at first difficult to believe she felt emotions. His first impression had been of someone trying to hide, to be inaccessible, but her remarks were so often candid and even intimate that he came to realize this could not be true. Instead, he discovered, it was simply that her nature had been formed in such a unique way that no matter how openly she verbalized her deepest feelings, she was unable to communicate those feelings in standard ways. Talking about her crushed dream of winning an Olympic gold medal, she did not sound crushed, so that even while she was speaking he'd almost overlooked the import of her words. It wasn't until later that he began to realize how truly devastated she must have been. Which was what confused him: He could not read her! She emitted no vibes. And if she did, they were on such a new and subtle frequency that he did not catch them, and this was what disturbed him. Threatened him, really, because all the while he felt she was reading *him* so easily. After three days he did not know her, and this despite her openness, consideration, friendliness even. One night she offered to cook dinner. "At my place," she said. A kindness? Or merely the suggestion of a possibility? And when he answered, "I thought I'd take you out to dinner," she responded, "Oh, don't trust my cooking, eh?" Was she annoyed, kidding, sexually rejected? WHAT? He did not know, which was why he'd suggested they switch their communicating to a more physical level—sports—where he, at thirty-three, still in shape, would feel on firmer ground. He'd decided on basketball because it was a sport with which he was still familiar and so might hold his own against her, not be humiliated, and also because the movements it required were similar to those of volleyball, a game he'd never played. Which was why, too, finally, he said, "I'd like to go one-on-one with you, Mary Jo."

"Really? And where?"

Eventually, he'd succeeded in communicating his desire to play basketball. "That would be a good match," she said. "Basically, there's no difference between us as far as size goes." (At dinner one night she'd worn a miniskirt and four-inch clogs. She took him by the arm and led him to their table. The other diners stared at her, "The Superstar," three inches taller and infinitely more visible than the man beside her.) He put down the receiver, for these arrangements had been made on the telephone, and stared at himself in the mirror. All those months of preparation, lifting weights even, and for what . . . "as far as size goes."

Under a hot desert sun that warmed and softened the paved basketball court, Mary Jo Peppler, dribbling with her left hand, backed in toward the basket. She moved left-right-left-right à la Earl Monroe. Behind her, at the foul line, her opponent pressed his hand against her buttocks (momentarily discombobulated by unexpected malleability) in that classic NBA defense designed to impede progress. She backed in closer. He bumped her with his chest. She pushed back with her buttocks. He restrained an urge to shove her with both hands and, instead, spread his legs and planted his feet firmly. She leaned backward. He pressed his chest against her back, his labored breathing in her right ear, where, suddenly, he smelled lilacs, was disoriented, grew slack, while she spun around him for an easy layup.

He had met her at her apartment that Sunday morning. She'd handed him a ten-speed racing bike, picked up her own bike with one hand (in the other she held a basketball) and carried it down the flight of stairs to the street. He tripped on the top step, tumbled down the stairs and landed in a tangle of spokes and handlebars at her feet. She looked down at him (her opponent?) and did not laugh. "Are you all right?" He smiled up at her and nodded. She tucked the basketball under her sweatshirt, looking immediately pregnant, and rode off. Within seconds she had far outdistanced him through the deserted El Paso streets. Hunched forward over the handlebars, she pedaled rhythmically, her long legs pumping without effort, it seemed, flesh-colored pistons glistening in the sunlight. He struggled and sweated but still the distance between them grew rapidly. Every so often he could see her legs stop pumping. She would straighten up, lift her face to the cool breeze, remain motionless for a long moment, coasting, savoring the fruits of her labor, and then suddenly hunch forward again to resume her pace.

She passed a Spanish-style church just as Mass was letting out. Startled parishoners, mostly Mexican-Americans, stared after the towering and apparently pregnant woman in shorts who was pedaling so single-mindedly down the street. She seemed not even to notice them, was no longer conscious of him either, of his following her, but had completely lost herself in the rhythmic and, to her, pleasurable pumping of her legs. He remembered Jim Brennand telling him about the professional bicycle racer they had hired to coach her for the Superstars competition. They'd gone to the University of Texas at El Paso campus, where the racer had asked her to take a spin around the track. "To see what you're doing wrong," he said. When she returned he told her, "You don't need me. You could go on the pro circuit right now." At both Houston and Rotunda she had won the bicycling events.

The score was tied now, and the next basket would win. They had been playing under the hot sun for almost an hour. She was not even breathing heavily, while he was exhausted. After every basket he doubled over in pain, clutched his stomach and gasped as if trying to draw breath from the pavement. Always the athlete, she was in shape in a way he'd never been. Her body had not been honed for any one particular skill—shooting a basketball or throwing a baseball—but was simply in generally fine physical shape. Healthy. It was a state she'd achieved naturally over the years through daily routines of weight lifting, calisthenics, jogging and bicycling, which she performed not necessarily in preparation for some special competition but just for the mental and physical exhilaration she experienced when her body was finely tuned.

"I listen to my body," she once told him. "I don't train my body to do anything that's not good for it. I don't drink coffee—it tastes like shit. I don't smoke. I don't like the taste of liquor so I don't drink it. But I'm not a health food nut, either. I'm just conscious about eating things that are good for me. I think when something goes wrong with your body it's because you have a negative attitude toward it and this manifests itself in some sickness. When I was nineteen, my dentist told me I had a cavity. I told him it was impossible. He showed me the X-ray. I went home and for a few weeks was very conscious of what I ate. When I went back to the dentist the cavity had disappeared. It's all part of controlling your body. It's O.K. to train your body to do things that are good for it, like running and calisthenics and things. I *feel* good when I do sports. My body feels good. I relax."

He had never been in such shape in his life. For him, sports had always been merely a collection of skills to be mastered for some upcoming competition. For instance, he had retained over the years an ability to shoot accurate long jump shots, a skill he used every so often to achieve victories over much younger men. Once that competition ceased, however, once victory was his (or defeat, in which case that skill became meaningless) he derived little satisfaction from it. In fact, quite the contrary was true. He was often mentally and physically drained beyond belief, as he was now in competition with her.

Still, he had controlled himself, at first. He played delicately enough, giving her plenty of room to maneuver, careful where he touched and reached, taking only long easy shots that required no close contact. To his surprise, however, she did not play so delicately. She played the kind of rough, physical game that he'd always delighted in. At times, unconsciously, she fouled blatantly, shoving him with both hands whenever he drove toward the basket. At one point he had stationed himself underneath the basket to retrieve her errant shot. As the ball bounced off the rim and he was ready to leap for it, he felt two knees in the small of his back. He lurched forward and tumbled onto the grass while, behind him, she tipped in her own shot. "You O.K.?"

she asked, without emotion. He smiled, looking up from
the grass. "Fine," he said.

The next time he got possession of the ball he began
backing in toward the basket. She tried to push him
forward but, with some effort, he was able to force her
back. Although she was strong, it was still a woman's
strength, not a man's, and he felt that he could manipu-
late her at will, exactly as he could any other man his
height but some twenty-five pounds lighter. When he
was close to the basket, he gave her a head fake, she left
the ground, he waited a split second and then went up
as she was coming down. He felt her jaw on his shoulder, heard a snap, and laid the ball in the basket. He
offered solicitations. She made exaggerated chewing
gestures with her mouth, said she was fine, and they
resumed play. They lost themselves again in the rough,
physical exertion they both were enjoying so much.
He'd forgotten completely that she was a woman. She
was simply his opponent now, whom he *had* to beat.
He tried to cheat her on the score, but she caught him.
Soaked with perspiration, he took off his shirt. "Trying
to turn me on?" she said, breaking his concentration
just enough so that she could score two successive bas-
kets.

She was an untutored basketball player. She did not
dribble or shoot very well and so was at a disadvantage
against him in a one-on-one competition. But she
moved beautifully, flowing like silk. She ran gracefully,
her toes pointed toward the ground like someone leap-

ing from rock to rock across a stream. And she seemed
to derive such pleasure from her movements, an almost
sensual pleasure that diffused over her face, lent it the
kind of unconscious and accessible glow he'd never noticed before. Still, she would have been more comfortable with teammates who could feed her the ball as she
rolled toward the hoop, catching it on upstretched
fingertips while simultaneously gliding upward, rising
to the bait in one easy motion and laying it in. Working
by herself, she had difficulty maneuvering with the ball,
and so the score had remained close. Now it was tied
and the next basket would win.

He wondered, should he win? What pale satisfaction
would he derive from beating a Superstar? A woman?
Was such a victory necessary to him? And what would
it tell? Assuredly more about himself than his opponent. Dribbling toward the basket, he pondered worth
and price and a myriad other possibilities, while his
opponent pushed and shoved him back, shoved him so
forcefully, in fact, that he momentarily forgot his conscious self, faked and jumped. *Good!* He experienced,
as always, the sensual flash that came instantly with
victory. But it faded quickly and was gone, replaced by
the exhausting realization that once more he had simply warded off defeat, for the time being. He collapsed
in the grass, gasping for breath.

She broke into a broad smile. "That was fantastic!"
she said. "I'd almost forgot how much fun basketball is.
It's a lot like volleyball, only some of the movements are

different. They're so pretty!" She sat beside him, still luxuriating in those movements, and for the first time in three days she began to talk with animation. "I'm intrigued by movement," she said. "I'm nearsighted, so when I think of certain people I don't see images, I see them only in the way they move. As a volleyball coach I never see plays as a series of x's and o's but as a sense of flow. Movement rather than words should be the prime communicator in any sport. A lot of times I like to go to the gym alone and just practice the different movements. I dive after an imaginary ball, leap in the air, and just enjoy all those movements. When I execute properly I get a great satisfaction that's independent of winning or losing. I guess this stems from all those years in volleyball when I was trying to win an Olympic gold medal. There were so many obstacles that I never even got close to my goal. The girls and I would practice six hours a day in a vacuum, never even approaching that medal. I'd tell them, 'That movement will never work against the Russians,' and all the while in the back of my mind was the thought, 'We'll probably never even *play* the Russians!'

"Soon perfection became our only goal. I think that's true of most women athletes. For so long we've been deprived of goals men are accustomed to achieving—money, recognition—that we've ceased to be goal-centered. For instance, when I ran the quarter mile at the Superstars competition I finished fifth, but it was the fastest time I'd ever run in my life. It was *my* best performance so it was one of the most satisfying moments in my life. More satisfying even than *winning* the Superstars, because there were a number of sports in it that I didn't feel were any true test of an athlete. Men compete differently, however. They're aggressive. Their satisfaction comes from dominating their opponent rather than striving toward perfection. Basically that's self-defeating, because if they lose they've got nothing from sport, and even if they win they've destroyed part of their own identity. Women are more protective than aggressive. At the Superstars we were all coaching one another even if it meant that coaching might turn around and beat us. Men wouldn't dare help another man who might beat them. They have this ego problem that women don't. I think women should continue to be coached toward perfection rather than one-upmanship, otherwise it will cause them an identity crisis. We don't like to dominate. We sublimate our aggressions rather than acting overtly, which creates a problem for women in sport. Acting overtly—aggressively—is supposed to be what sport is all about. At least, that's what men have told us.

"Sport has been a male domain for so long that it's the men who have defined how one should compete. The problem for the woman athlete is that we've accepted these definitions and tried to copy them. But since it's not consistent with our natures, the best we can become is just a poor copy of aggressive male models. Like Billy Jean, for instance. But there's a point at which you can always crack a copy. What women need to do is redefine sport in feminine terms, terms more consistent with our natures and yet which still bring out our best. Women aren't very good at one-upmanship, but we are unbelievably persevering—the endurance of women in the face of problems is phenomenal—and very competitive within ourselves. For instance, when I get dressed up to go out I have to look the best I can. *My* best! But I never feel in competition with another woman I might be with. Trying to show up another woman is male-oriented. For a woman to compete like that is living a lie.

"Usually when a woman goes into sport she has this crisis of whether to adopt certain male traits or try to remain feminine. All women in sport have certain masculine traits—they walk like men, or something. Chrissie Evert is an exception, but I think it's something she works very hard at. You know, trying to be ultrafeminine as a defense mechanism. Anyway, when this crisis develops in women they have to make a choice. Either sport suffers or their femininity suffers. Supposedly sport makes a man of a boy, right? But can sport make a woman of a girl? Usually it's the opposite that's true —it makes something masculine of a woman. But it shouldn't. Women should be able to compete in such a way that it complements their nature rather than compromises it. We have things we can receive from sport as well as give to it that are different from what men offer and receive. Finesse and a striving for perfection as opposed to strength and aggressiveness. Women's volleyball, for example, is much more exciting than the men's because it has so much more finesse. Still, it's exciting to watch power, too. There should be a place for both. That would be a beautiful thing. A woman could then become more feminine in sport rather than having to surrender her femininity. Of course, most women aren't even aware of having to make such a choice. But they should be. They must recognize these forces working against them so as not to slide unconsciously into certain roles not compatible with their nature. I think I have a solid idea of what femininity is, and it's not dependent on any male definition. A lot of female athletes have to have marriage and kids in order to rationalize that they're still feminine and in sport. They have to have their femininity verified outside themselves. For most women, it's men who define what 'feminine' really means. I don't need that. Femininity should exist in itself, should be independent of male attitudes. I'm glad to be both a woman and an athlete. There are things about being a woman that I love. Of course, I realize that any woman who wants to be successful as something other than a housewife or mother has to fight certain social forces. But I don't live in a world of such forces. I feel that I'm outside normal society.

"Sport makes me independent. I live pretty much in my own world. I don't know whether or not it's a defense mechanism, but I never feel the pressures of the world. I miss a lot of things. As a coach I didn't pick up on a lot of petty jealousies between players on my team. I guess that's because I was dealing with ideals and ideas, which may have been a fault in my coaching. I'm more a passive than an active person. I don't know how I evolved, really. I'm not personally competitive in a one-on-one sense. I have no desire to dominate anyone. Lately, I've been trying to analyze what forces motivate me. It's not money. After my Superstars victory I could have renegotiated my Sols' contract, but I didn't. What's the difference between another $50,000 or $100,000, when you already have enough to live comfortably? The rest is frosting. I'm not motivated by recognition either. Fame turns me off. It means less privacy. I don't need someone to tell me how wonderful I am. If I didn't feel I was wonderful ten years ago, I wouldn't have been playing in empty gyms for six hours a day. I've established my ego strokes somewhere along the way and I'm secure now."

Mary Jo Peppler is sitting on a sofa in a small room off the lobby of the KELP-TV studios on the outskirts of El Paso. Sitting across from her on a straight-backed chair is Bob Nisberg, a KELP-TV sportscaster, who is preparing her for her appearance on his 8 P.M. sports show, which will be aired in approximately fifteen minutes.

She is lightly made up with eye shadow and lipstick. She is wearing a figured Qiana blouse, a yellow suit with a short jacket and knee-length skirt, tan-colored stockings and high-heeled pumps. Her legs are crossed and her hands are laid one over the other on her knee. She is alternately talking, smiling, listening and occasionally gesturing with her hands. She looks less like a famous athlete than she does some tall suburban housewife who is president of the Coronado High School PTA. Or maybe some precise, clipped, self-assured businesswoman from downtown El Paso who seems not the least bit flustered by the fact that she will shortly appear on television.

Nisberg is a small man dressed in a bold plaid sportsjacket. He is wearing dark-rimmed eyeglasses. His arms are folded across his chest as if protecting himself, and his legs are crossed like hers. A clipboard with some papers is balanced on his lap. He reads from these papers in a monotonous voice, only rarely looking up to glance at his guest. And when he does look up, his glance is invariably off-center, a bit to her right, so that he seems to be peering directly over her right shoulder. Reading from the clipboard, he asks a question about future endorsements.

"Possibly I'll do a 'No-nonsense' pantyhose commercial," she says, and then adds with an abrupt, snorting laugh, "You know, me and Namath with our legs intertwined." Nisberg does not smile until he hears her laugh. Then he smiles faintly, without looking up, and asks the next question. She answers more seriously now.

"I feel women athletes are more interesting at this

point in history than they ever will be again. Everything that's happening to us is new." Before she finishes her answer Nisberg begins his next question. His voice cuts off her final two words. He seems, like some technological marvel to be functioning smoothly, as programmed, but only the slightest bit out of sync. She stares at him a long moment before finally smiling again and saying, "I'm supposed to be on the 'Tonight Show' with MacLean Stevenson. We're going to have a Superstars competition."

"What if he beats you?" Nisberg asks.

"Then he can call himself Superwoman." Again that snorting laugh, as Nisberg turns back a paper and begins reading his next question.

Later, sitting on plastic chairs on a raised platform, Mary Jo Peppler and Bob Nisberg face a battery of television cameras and wait for their cue. Off to their right a tall blonde woman in a blue dress is standing in front of a weather map of the United States. Her face, fine-boned and pale, is expressionless, but her hands are performing an intricate ballet, weaving in the air like fingered snakes, beckoning, imploring like those of an ancient sorceress as she conveys the weather report in sign language to her deaf viewers. Finally she stops and the cue is given to Nisberg. He reads a short introduction and then asks his guest her first question. Smiling directly at the camera she says, "I never really made a choice, Bob. I just always was an athlete. . . ."

Leaving the studio an hour later, she hands the

writer her car keys. "You drive, O.K?" She waits for him to open the door for her. "I'm not very good at this," she adds. "Jim (Brennand) is always getting on me. He says I just charge through doors without waiting. I've got to be more ladylike, he says. It's all part of the image—'understated elegance.'" And she laughs her distinctive laugh. The first time the writer heard that laugh was when he and Mary Jo, Smitty-Duke and his wife, and Jim Brennand and his wife had driven across the border to Juarez to have dinner at the Costa del Sol restaurant. They were sitting at a long table being hovered over by Mexican waiters in dinner jackets, when Brennand made a joke. Everyone laughed. But Mary Jo's abrupt, snorting laugh drowned out the rest. The writer was very conscious of her laugh then, surrounded by the wives, but with time, and without others around, he'd grown accustomed to it. It did not seem so loud and jarring anymore. In fact, it was now so natural to him that, when in the presence of the wives again, he found their demure laughter grating.

It is dark as they drive through the desert toward El Paso. She says, "Wasn't he something? He was so up-tight. He couldn't even look me in the eye. I tried to put him at ease but he just wouldn't loosen up. I have this part of my personality, I don't know what it is really, but I have a problem relating to men. A lot of men feel threatened by me. I don't feel we're in competition or anything, but they seem to. Guys, mostly athletes, will take me out and try . . . you know, try to get something going. And all the while I have this feeling they want to conquer me, not know me. It's like a way of diminishing me, my size and my athletic ability. I think that was one of my problems with the USVBA, too. They were mostly older men, administrators not athletes, and they felt threatened by me. They didn't know what motivated me—hell, even I'm not sure—and so they didn't know how to handle me. If you know what motivates a person you can handle them. Even Jim (Brennand) and Wayne (Vandenberg) aren't sure what motivates me. They can't predict what I'll do in terms of their world.

"Last week the IVA put out a quote supposedly from me. I was quoted as saying after my Superstars victory, "Bring on Bob Seagren!" That's ridiculous! Hell, I'm not interested in any one-on-one competition with men. The quote went on to say that I wanted to win a Superstars competition of all the men and women athletes. That's against my whole philosophy. I was so mad I tore up the office. They were all shook up. I don't know why, but people—men, usually—always feel that they're qualified to speak for me. After I was beaten in the 60-yard dash at Houston, Wayne told the press I had been psyched out. And that made me mad. Not that he got it wrong, but that he felt qualified to speak for me. People are always trying to represent my thoughts and attitudes without understanding my motivations. In the USVBA there was always some administrator speaking for the women athletes. Those women's whole lives revolved around sport, but they were never asked what they thought.

"Anyway, because of these things I was, at first, afraid to turn pro with the Sols. I didn't know how I'd get along with the men. With Smitty, for instance. I don't know. He tries to be open with me, but he still keeps up his defenses. I can't loosen up with him. He has a reputation for having this really strong ego, you know, and yet we practiced recently and the funny thing was, he was setting me up for spikes instead of looking for them for himself. He subjugated himself to my game. It really surprised me. I'm looking forward to pro volleyball now. The new rules are intellectually stimulating. And the men are so much stronger, too. That's physically stimulating. There are guys in sport who have achieved superstar status with builds not much different than mine. I think there is a place I could have in male sport, although I never desired it. I still don't, other than the satisfaction I get from being challenged physically on a higher level than before. With the women I've tried not to be as physical these last few years. At times I was so strong I intimidated my own teammates. They were awed by my strength, which never seemed to be anything much to me. I get no ego satisfaction from it. Anyway, I felt it would be better for the team if I pulled myself out of the power part of the game. I let the younger girls do the power playing and I became a setter. I relied more on finesse, which should help me in the IVA."

As they reach the El Paso city limits, she says, "Turn left here. I want to show you something." They drive up a winding hill and suddenly are on a high plateau overlooking all of El Paso. The city, in darkness, spreads out in every direction as far as the eye can see. It is visible only as an endless desert dotted with widely spaced lights. Far behind the city, rising like a dark, jagged curtain, are the Rocky Mountains. "Isn't it something," she says. "I've never seen the sky such a big thing before. And all that space. Sometimes I just drive out into the country and it goes on and on and on. I feel so big in this space. I belong to it. I flow into it. Sometimes I feel . . . I feel my body has no limitations in all this space."

Wearing slacks and a man's double-breasted trench-coat, Mary Jo Peppler is walking through Dallas International Airport on her way to the flight that will take her to New York City. There she will spend four days in a constant round of luncheons, dinners, promotions, business meetings and television appearances, all rewards of her Superstar victory. It is a prospect she is not looking forward to. She does not like to leave El Paso and her newfound permanence, especially not for a city like New York, where, she fears, she will not be on firm ground. Already she is worried about New York taxis and the proper amount one should tip. She is also worried that New York, unlike El Paso, is no haven for outlaws. Nor is it spacious and open. No one says of New

York that their body feels without limitations there. Her biggest fear, however, is that New York will be just like Los Angeles.

"I hated L.A.," she says. "When I was growing up there I would rather have lived anywhere else in the world. It's so phony. There are no sincere people you can relate to. There are only cults, and people trying to fit themselves into one. It's a monster that gobbles you up and spits you out. I always get lost there, have these unbelievably frustrating experiences. I don't ever feel I'm in control of myself in L.A."

As she walks, some people stop and stare while others just glance curiously as they hurry toward their flights. Some recognize her immediately and break into a broad smile, while to others she is someone they should know but can't quite place. Still others merely look after her because she is such a tall, attractive woman.

In El Paso Mary Jo was instantly recognized. People shouted to her on the street, "Heh, Superstar!" and she waved back. In restaurants, young children, always girls between the ages of nine and twelve, walked over to her table, hesitated a moment, their heads lowered, then thrust a piece of paper and a pen at her. Unused to such adulation, she merely signed the paper without comment. The young girls remained there, waiting for a benediction, a blessing, anything, while around the room the expectant eyes of every diner were on them. Finally she would smile at the girl and ask a question, "Do you like sports?" or "How old are you?" or "What school do you go to?" all of which would be delivered in an abrupt, clipped tone, without a hint of interest or warmth. Unlike other athletes more accustomed to fame and its demands, she had not mastered that deceptive art of feigned interest, probably never will, probably would find it to much of a strain against her nature to ever toss her arm over the shoulder of an adoring fan, hug that child and say, grinning, "Why you're really a big girl for your age. I'll bet you're some kinda athlete, eh? Beat all the boys in baseball and everything?"

Only occasionally does her recognition have unpleasant aspects. One night in El Paso at a restaurant that was frequented by couples and singles in their midtwenties—denims, Pumas and floral shirts—she was accosted by a young man. He was standing at the bar with a few couples. "Heh, you're the Superstar?" She smiled. "Whatcha gonna do with all that money, huh?" She said, "I'm gonna spend it, I guess." He replied, "Why dontcha give me some?" She said "I don't think I could do that," and continued into the dining room. Behind her, the man whispered something to his friends and they looked after her and laughed.

Mary Jo stops at an American Airlines ticket counter and pushes her ticket across the counter to the agent, a short man in a blue sportsjacket with a winged insignia on his lapel. "Be with you gentlemen in a minute," he says, without looking up from the counter. "A fine day to travel, isn't it, gentlemen? And just where are you gentlemen headed for today?" She stares at the top of his balding head without anger or embarassment, half-smiling to herself.

It is five o'clock in the afternoon on a cold, blustery spring day. Outside the Regency Hotel on Park Avenue a group of chauffeurs mill about on the sidewalk. They are identically dressed in black caps, white shirts, black ties, black suits and black shoes. Passing time, they smoke, blow into their cold hands, make small-talk with the doorman or merely lounge against their black limousines. Behind the three gold fleur-de-lis painted on the plate-glass window of the Regency Bar, their employers are having a late afternoon cocktail.

The room is packed with well-dressed New Yorkers —mostly middle-aged men in dark, vested, pin-striped suits and their much younger companions in silky knee-length dresses. Standing at the crowded bar, two young women are talking to a pencil-thin black man in a tightly fitted suit. The women are poised on either side of him like identical bookends, and as they talk they alternately blow smoke toward the ceiling and glance distractedly over the black man's shoulders. Seated at one of the white leather booths against the wall is an older man with two young women seated on either side of him. All three face the crowded room. They are blank, silent, frozen, but perfectly visible. At one of the small cocktail tables in the middle of the room, another middle-aged man is talking intimately across the table to a woman wearing black eye liner that makes her eyes look like those of a raccoon. She bears a striking resemblance to the late Jacqueline Susann. They are holding hands across the table.

At the table beside them, Mary Jo Peppler, still wearing her trenchcoat, sips from a glass of beer and says, without lasciviousness, "Trying to turn us on, I guess." She lowers her head for a moment, then lifts it. "I have no emotional attachments. I've never been tempted to be married. Oh, you run into someone you can talk to once in a while, but then you never see them again; or else you do and after knowing them they let you down. I've given up hope of ever finding someone."

Behind her, seated in a booth against the wall, a woman in a black dress is talking into a silver-plated telephone. "It was Ashley," she says. Then, exasperated, she repeats emphatically, "D-A-V-I-D Ashley. The producer!"

"You get married," says Mary Jo, "and there are all those social patterns to follow. You belong to someone. I don't know. I'm too independent. Most emotional attachments are so dependent. 'Oh, I'm so hurt you didn't call!' That type of thing. I don't want someone being dependent on me, either. I'm a very giving person, but I don't like to get things back. Then I feel obligated to people. When I was a child I always used to do things for my mother, the dishes and stuff, because I could see how it pleased her. It's kind of a hangup in my life. I'm very good at recognizing what makes people happy and I try to give it to them. But there's a point with pleasing people when you make them dependent on you. It becomes a vicious circle. The girls on the volleyball team, for instance. They drained me. I helped a lot of them in regards to their femininity, but there came a point when, unless they had my approval, they couldn't go on. It's like with my younger sister. She had some problems awhile ago and so she came to live with me. I helped her out and now she's doing fine. When my parents saw that, they began to look at me differently. For five years after I left home they wouldn't talk to me, and then they began to look to me for strength. My mother's getting a divorce now from my father. She's in a terrible state. She wants me to give her strength. I think it's wrong to let people be dependent on you. There's a point they have to do it alone. But once you get into those relationships, it's very hard to train people out of them. That's why I don't think I'll ever have any emotional attachments. You just never find people who don't want to be dependent on you or have you dependent on them."

Standing at the bar, a middle-aged blonde holds up her arm and the gold lamé pocketbook dangling from it, for the inspection of a friend. In a French accent she says, "It's from Cartiers, dear." She is smoking a small cigar and drinking brandy from a large glass. She looks around the room and says, "The Regency is so smart. It's the smartest place in town."

After four days of New York luncheons, dinners, plays, promotions, photographing sessions, business meetings and a television appearance on the "AM America" Show, Mary Jo Peppler leaves the city for a visit to the Connecticut suburbs. She arrives late in the evening. The children—three girls, two boys—had waited up expectantly for her arrival but have long since succumbed to sleep. Only the writer and his wife are still awake. She looks different. She is wearing a fur coat. Her hair has been styled and her face heavily made up. "For a cover photograph for *The Ladies' Home Journal,*" says Mary Jo. "The photographer, he had a French name, François or something, said he had to redo me. I wasn't right, he said. I should lose some weight, too. That's just what I need, right? Become a 118-pound model. I wouldn't even be able to lift a volleyball."

When Mary Jo wakes the following morning she washes off her makeup and appears downstairs for breakfast wearing a t-shirt, jeans and nothing on her feet. The children trot out one by one to meet her. She smiles at each, says hello, what's your name and that is all. She also meets the writer's mother-in-law, who is helping her daughter prepare the Saturday morning breakfast. Mary Jo has only a roll and a glass of milk, and then asks her host if he would mind if she worked out with his weights which she sees laid out by a window in the dining room.

"Of course not," he says. "I'll lighten them for you."

She picks up a dumbbell weighing about twenty pounds, hefts it in her hand, and says, "That's O.K. I think I can handle these." She begins doing bicep curls by the window which looks out on the backyard littered with a rusted swing set, a red tricycle and a broken sandbox. Mary Jo is facing the window but sees nothing. Her eyes have a distant, almost catatonic look as she struggles with the weights.

In the kitchen three generations of women go about their Saturday morning. The grandmother, in her late fifties, cleans off the table. She scrapes the remnants of food into the garbage pail and then begins to wash the dishes. She whispers to her daughter, "So pretty! Is she married?" The mother, in her thirties, shakes her head no. She is measuring out medicine into a plastic spoon and trying to force it down the throat of her four-year-old son. The third generation, an oldest daughter of twelve, is pacing around the kitchen waiting anxiously for Mary Jo to finish with her weights so she can talk to her. She, too, is an athlete, strong-willed and, of all the children, had most anticipated Mary Jo's arrival. She is 5'7" and will be the first girl in town to make the Little League. Today, however, she does not look like an athlete. She is wearing a sweater, a miniskirt, stockings and clogs—the same outfit she had worn out to dinner with her father a few nights before.

Now in the kitchen, the daughter fidgets with her skirt and waits. Finally she can restrain herself no longer. She peeks around the refrigerator into the dining room. Mary Jo is lying on the floor doing sit-ups with a weight grasped behind her head. Sweating, she struggles upward, at the same time exhaling and blowing wisps of hair off her forehead. The young girl stares in fascination. The grandmother continues washing the dishes. Her daughter tightens the cap on the medicine bottle. Mary Jo struggles upward for another sit-up as the young girl continues to stare at her—transfixed, hypnotized by the sudden unfolding of such infinite possibilities.